NEW SELECTED POEMS

Paul Muldoon was born in County Armagh in 1951. He read
English at Queen's University, Belfast, and while he was at
university Faber and Faber published his first collection of
poems. His most recent collection, *The Annals of Chile* (1994),
won the T. S. Eliot Memorial Prize and was a Poetry Book
Society Choice. *New Selected Poems* was the winner of the
1997 Irish Times Irish Literature Prize for Poetry. In 1987 he
moved to the United States; he is a Professor at Princeton
University.

PAUL MULDOON

New Selected Poems
1968–1994

faber and faber
LONDON · BOSTON

First published in 1996
by Faber and Faber Limited
3 Queen Square London WC1N 3AU

Phototypeset by Wilmasct Ltd, Wirall
Printed and bound in Great Britain by
Mackays of Chatham PLC, Chatham, Kent

A CIP record for this book
is available from the British Library

ISBN 0-571-17784-0 (pbk)
ISBN 0-571-17953-3 (cased)

4 6 8 10 9 7 5 3

Contents

Dancers at the Moy

This Italian square
And circling plain
Black once with mares
And their stallions,
The flat Blackwater
Turning its stones

Over hour after hour
As their hooves shone
And lifted together
Under the black rain,
One or other Greek war
Now coloured the town

Blacker than ever before
With hungry stallions
And their hungry mares
Like hammocks of skin,
The flat Blackwater
Unable to contain

Itself as horses poured
Over acres of grain
In a black and gold river.
No band of Athenians
Arrived at the Moy fair
To buy for their campaign,

Peace having been declared
And a treaty signed.
The black and gold river
Ended as a trickle of brown
Where those horses tore
At briars and whins,

Ate the flesh of each other
Like people in famine.
The flat Blackwater
Hobbled on its stones
With a wild stagger
And sag in its backbone,

The local people gathered
Up the white skeletons.
Horses buried for years
Under the foundations
Give their earthen floors
The ease of trampolines.

February

He heard that in Derryscollop there is a tree
For every day of the year,
And the extra tree is believed to grow
One year in every four.

He had never yet taken time to grieve
For this one without breasts
Or that one wearing her heart on her sleeve
Or another with her belly slashed.

He had never yet taken time to love
The blind pink fledgeling fallen out of the nest
Of one sleeping with open mouth
And her head at a list.

What was he watching and waiting for,
Walking Scollop every day?
For one intending to leave at the end of the year,
Who would break the laws of time and stay.

The Electric Orchard

The early electric people had domesticated the wild ass.
They knew all about falling off.
Occasionally, they would have fallen out of the trees.
Climbing again, they had something to prove
To their neighbours. And they did have neighbours.
The electric people lived in villages
Out of their need of security and their constant hunger.
Together they would divert their energies

To neutral places. Anger to the banging door,
Passion to the kiss.
And electricity to earth. Having stolen his thunder
From an angry god, through the trees
They had learned to string his lightning.
The women gathered random sparks into their aprons,
A child discovered the swing
Among the electric poles. Taking everything as given,

The electric people were confident, hardly proud.
They kept fire in a bucket,
Boiled water and dry leaves in a kettle, watched the lid
By the blue steam lifted and lifted.
So that, where one of the electric people happened to fall,
It was accepted as an occupational hazard.
There was something necessary about the thing. The North Wall
Of the Eiger was notorious for blizzards,

If one fell there his neighbour might remark, Bloody fool.
All that would have been inappropriate,
Applied to the experienced climber of electric poles.
I have achieved this great height?
No electric person could have been that proud,
Thirty or forty feet. Perhaps not that,
If the fall happened to be broken by the roof of a shed.
The belt would burst, the call be made,

The ambulance arrive and carry the faller away
To hospital with a scream.
There and then the electric people might invent the railway,
Just watching the lid lifted by the steam.
Or decide that all laws should be based on that of gravity,
Just thinking of the faller fallen.
Even then they were running out of things to do and see.
Gradually, they introduced legislation

Whereby they nailed a plaque to every last electric pole.
They would prosecute any trespassers.
The high up, singing and live fruit liable to shock or kill
Were forbidden. Deciding that their neighbours
And their neighbours' innocent children ought to be stopped
For their own good, they threw a fence
Of barbed wire round the electric poles. None could describe
Electrocution, falling, the age of innocence.

Wind and Tree

In the way that the most of the wind
Happens where there are trees,

Most of the world is centred
About ourselves.

Often where the wind has gathered
The trees together,

One tree will take
Another in her arms and hold.

Their branches that are grinding
Madly together,

It is no real fire.
They are breaking each other.

Often I think I should be like
The single tree, going nowhere,

Since my own arm could not and would not
Break the other. Yet by my broken bones

I tell new weather.

Thrush

I guessed the letter
    Must be yours. I recognized
The cuttle ink,
    The serif on
The P. I read the postmark and the date,
    Impatience held
By a paperweight.
    I took your letter at eleven
To the garden
    With my tea.
And suddenly the yellow gum secreted
    Halfway up
The damson bush
    Had grown a shell.
I let those scentless pages fall
    And took it
In my feckless hand. I turned it over
    On its back
To watch your mouth
    Withdraw. Making a lean, white fist
Out of my freckled hand.

The Waking Father

My father and I are catching spricklies
Out of the Oona river.
They have us feeling righteous,
The way we have thrown them back.
Our benevolence is astounding.

When my father stood out in the shallows
It occurred to me that
The spricklies might have been piranhas,
The river a red carpet
Rolling out from where he had just stood,

Or I wonder now if he is dead or sleeping.
For if he is dead I would have his grave
Secret and safe,
I would turn the river out of its course,
Lay him in its bed, bring it round again.

        No one would question
That he had treasures or his being a king,
Telling now of the real fish farther down.

The Cure for Warts

Had I been the seventh son of a seventh son
Living at the dead centre of a wood
Or at the dead end of a lane,
I might have cured by my touch alone
That pair of warts nippling your throat,

Who had no faith in a snail rubbed on your skin
And spiked on a thorn like a king's head,
In my spittle on shrunken stone,
In bathing yourself at the break of dawn
In dew or the black cock's or the bull's blood,

In other such secrets told by way of a sign
Of the existence of one or other god,
So I doubt if any woman's son
Could have cured by his touch alone
That pair of warts nibbling your throat.

Good Friday, 1971. Driving Westward

It was good going along with the sun
Through Ballygawley, Omagh and Strabane.
I started out as it was getting light
And caught sight of hares all along the road
That looked to have been taking a last fling,
Doves making the most of their offerings
As if all might not be right with the day

Where I moved through morning towards the sea.
I was glad that I would not be alone.
Those children who travel badly as wine
Waved as they passed in their uppity cars
And now the first cows were leaving the byres,
The first lorry had delivered its load.
A whole country was fresh after the night

Though people were still fighting for the last
Dreams and changing their faces where I paused
To read the first edition of the truth.
I gave a lift to the girl out of love
And crossed the last great frontier at Lifford.
Marooned by an iffing and butting herd
Of sheep, Letterkenny had just then laid

Open its heart and we passed as new blood
Back into the grey flesh of Donegal.
The sky went out of its way for the hills
And life was changing down for the sharp bends
Where the road had put its thin brown arm round
A hill and held on tight out of pure fear.
Errigal stepped out suddenly in our

Path and the thin arm tightened round the waist
Of the mountain and for a time I lost
Control and she thought we hit something big
But I had seen nothing, perhaps a stick
Lying across the road. I glanced back once
And there was nothing but a heap of stones.
We had just dropped in from nowhere for lunch

In Gaoth Dobhair, I happy and she convinced
Of the death of more than lamb or herring.
She stood up there and then, face full of drink,
And announced that she and I were to blame
For something killed along the way we came.
Children were warned that it was rude to stare,
Left with their parents for a breath of air.

Hedgehog

The snail moves like a
Hovercraft, held up by a
Rubber cushion of itself,
Sharing its secret

With the hedgehog. The hedgehog
Shares its secret with no one.
We say, Hedgehog, come out
Of yourself and we will love you.

We mean no harm. We want
Only to listen to what
You have to say. We want
Your answers to our questions.

The hedgehog gives nothing
Away, keeping itself to itself.
We wonder what a hedgehog
Has to hide, why it so distrusts.

We forget the god
Under this crown of thorns.
We forget that never again
Will a god trust in the world.

The Upriver Incident

He thanked his parents for keeping still
And left them sleeping, deaf and blind
After their heavy meal,

Then stole away where the moon was full
And the dogs gave no sound.
He thanked the dogs for keeping still

And ran along the tops of the dark hills
That heaped like the sleeping anaconda
After its heavy meal,

To the bright square in the highest coil
That was the lady's window.
She thanked her parents for keeping still

And they ran together over a further hill
Like the lady's belly so hard and round
After its heavy meal,

Till they stood at the top of the waterfall,
Its deep pool where they drowned.
Let us thank waters for not keeping still
After their heavy meal.

The Field Hospital

Taking, giving back their lives
By the strength of our bare hands,
By the silence of our knives,
We answer to no grey South

Nor blue North, not self defence,
The lie of just wars, neither
Cold nor hot blood's difference
In their discharging of guns,

But that hillside of fresh graves.
Would this girl brought to our tents
From whose flesh we have removed
Shot that George, on his day off,

Will use to weight fishing lines,
Who died screaming for ether,
Yet protest our innocence?
George lit the lanterns, in danced

Those gigantic, yellow moths
That brushed right over her wounds,
Pinning themselves to our sleeves
Like medals given the brave.

The Year of the Sloes, for Ishi

In the Moon
Of Frost in the Tepees,
There were two stars
That got free.
They yawned and stretched
To white hides,
One cutting a slit
In the wall of itself
And stepping out into the night.

In the Moon
Of the Dark Red Calf,
It had learned
To track itself
By following the dots
And dashes of its blood.
It knew the silence
Deeper
Than that of birds not singing.

In the Moon
Of the Snowblind,
The other fed the fire
At its heart
With the dream of a deer
Over its shoulder.
One water would wade through another,
Shivering,
Salmon of Knowledge leap the Fall.

In the Moon
Of the Red Grass Appearing,
He discovered her
Lying under a bush.
There were patches of yellowed
Snow and ice
Where the sun had not looked.
He helped her over the Black Hills
To the Ford of the Two Friends.

In the Moon
Of the Ponies Shedding,
He practised counting coups,
Knowing it harder
To live at the edge of the earth
Than its centre.
He caught the nondescript horse
And stepped
Down onto the prairies.

In the Moon
Of Making the Fat,
He killed his first bison.
Her quick knife ran under the skin
And offered the heart
To the sky.
They had been the horizon.
She saved what they could not eat
That first evening.

In the Moon
Of the Red Cherries,
She pledged that she would stay
So long as there would be
The Two Legged
And the Four Legged Ones,
Long as grass would grow and water
Flow, and the wind blow.
None of these things had forgotten.

In the Moon
Of the Black Cherries,
While he was looking for a place
To winter,
He discovered two wagons
Lying side by side
That tried to be a ring.
There were others in blue shirts
Felling trees for a square.

In the Moon
When the Calf Grows Hair,
There was a speck in the sky
Where he had left the tepee.
An eagle had started
Out of her side
And was waiting to return.
The fire was not cold,
The feet of six horses not circles.

In the Moon
Of the Season Changing,
He left the river
Swollen with rain.
He kicked sand over the fire.
He prepared his breast
By an ochre
That none would see his blood.
Any day now would be good to die.

In the Moon
Of the Leaves Falling,
I had just taken a bite out of the
Moon and pushed the plate
Of the world away.
Someone was asking for six troopers
Who had lain down
One after another
To drink a shrieking river.

In the Moon
Of the Trees Popping, two snails
Glittered over a dead Indian.
I realized that if his brothers
Could be persuaded to lie still,
One beside the other
Right across the Great Plains,
Then perhaps something of this original
Beauty would be retained.

Ned Skinner

Was 'a barbaric yawp',
If you took Aunt Sarah at her word.
He would step over the mountain
Of a summer afternoon
To dress a litter of pigs
On my uncle's farm.

Aunt Sarah would keep me in,
Taking me on her lap
Till it was over.
Ned Skinner wiped his knife
And rinsed his hands
In the barrel at the door-step.

He winked, and gripped my arm.
'It doesn't hurt, not so's you'd notice,
And God never slams one door
But another's lying open.
Them same pigs can see the wind.'
My uncle had given him five shillings.

Ned Skinner came back
While my uncle was in the fields.
'Sarah,' he was calling, 'Sarah.
You weren't so shy in our young day.
You remember yon time in Archer's loft?'
His face blazed at the scullery window.
'Remember? When the hay was won.'

Aunt Sarah had the door on the snib.
'That's no kind of talk
To be coming over. Now go you home.'
Silence. Then a wheeze.
We heard the whiskey-jug
Tinkle, his boots diminish in the yard.
Aunt Sarah put on a fresh apron.

The Mixed Marriage

My father was a servant-boy.
When he left school at eight or nine
He took up billhook and loy
To win the ground he would never own.

My mother was the school-mistress,
The world of Castor and Pollux.
There were twins in her own class.
She could never tell which was which.

She had read one volume of Proust,
He knew the cure for farcy.
I flitted between a hole in the hedge
And a room in the Latin Quarter.

When she had cleared the supper-table
She opened *The Acts of the Apostles*,
Aesop's Fables, Gulliver's Travels.
Then my mother went on upstairs

And my father further dimmed the light
To get back to hunting with ferrets
Or the factions of the faction-fights,
The Ribbon Boys, the Caravats.

Ma

Old photographs would have her bookish, sitting
Under a willow. I take that to be a croquet
Lawn. She reads aloud, no doubt from Rupert Brooke.
The month is always May or June.

Or with the stranger on the motor-bike.
Not my father, no. This one's all crew-cut
And polished brass buttons.
An American soldier, perhaps.
                                    And the full moon
Swaying over Keenaghan, the orchards and the cannery,
Thins to a last yellow-hammer, and goes.
The neighbours gather, all Keenaghan and Collegelands,
There is story-telling. Old miners at Coalisland
Going into the ground. Swinging, for fear of the gas,
The soft flame of a canary.

The Big House

I was only the girl under the stairs
But I was the first to notice something was wrong.
I was always first up and about, of course.
Those hens would never lay two days running
In the same place. I would rise early
And try round the haggard for fresh nests.
The mistress let me keep the egg-money.

And that particular night there were guests,
Mrs de Groot from the bridge set
And a young man who wrote stories for children,
So I wanted everything to be just right
When they trooped down to breakfast that morning.

I slept at the very top of that rambling house,
A tiny room with only a sky-light window.
I had brushed my hair and straightened my dress
And was just stepping into the corridor
When it struck me. That old boarded-up door
Was flung open. A pile of rubble and half-bricks
Was strewn across the landing floor.

I went on down. I was stooping among the hay-stacks
When there came a clatter of hooves in the yard.
The squire's sure-footed little piebald mare
Had found her own way home, as always.
He swayed some. Then fell headlong on the cobbles.

There was not so much as the smell of whiskey on him.
People still hold he had died of fright,
That the house was haunted by an elder brother
Who was murdered for his birthright.
People will always put two and two together.

What I remember most of that particular morning
Was how calmly everyone took the thing.
The mistress insisted that life would go on quietly
As it always had done. Breakfast was served
At nine exactly. I can still hear Mrs de Groot
Telling how she had once bid seven hearts.
The young man's stories were for grown-ups, really.

Lunch with Pancho Villa

I

'Is it really a revolution, though?'
I reached across the wicker table
With another $10,000 question.
My celebrated pamphleteer,
Co-author of such volumes
As *Blood on the Rose,*
The Dream and the Drums,
And *How It Happened Here,*
Would pour some untroubled Muscatel
And settle back in his cane chair.

'Look, son. Just look around you.
People are getting themselves killed
Left, right and centre
While you do what? Write rondeaux?
There's more to living in this country
Than stars and horses, pigs and trees,
Not that you'd guess it from your poems.
Do you never listen to the news?
You want to get down to something true,
Something a little nearer home.'

I called again later that afternoon,
A quiet suburban street.
'You want to stand back a little
When the world's at your feet.'
I'd have liked to have heard some more
Of his famous revolution.

I rang the bell, and knocked hard
On what I remembered as his front door,
That opened then, as such doors do,
Directly on to a back yard.

II

Not any back yard, I'm bound to say,
And not a thousand miles away
From here. No one's taken in, I'm sure,
By such a mild invention.
But where (I wonder myself) do I stand,
In relation to a table and chair,
The quince-tree I forgot to mention,
That suburban street, the door, the yard –
All made up as I went along
As things that people live among.

And such a person as lived there!
My celebrated pamphleteer!
Of course, I gave it all away
With those preposterous titles.
The Bloody Rose? The Dream and the Drums?
The three-day-wonder of the flowering plum!
Or was I desperately wishing
To have been their other co-author,
Or, at least, to own a first edition
Of *The Boot Boys and Other Battles?*

'When are you going to tell the truth?'
For there's no such book, so far as I know,
As *How it Happened Here*,
Though there may be. There may.

What should I say to this callow youth
Who learned to write last winter –
One of those correspondence courses –
And who's coming to lunch today?
He'll be rambling on, no doubt,
About pigs and trees, stars and horses.

Our Lady of Ardboe

I

Just there, in a corner of the whin-field,
Just where the thistles bloom.
She stood there as in Bethlehem
One night in nineteen fifty-three or four.

The girl leaning over the half-door
Saw the cattle kneel, and herself knelt.

II

I suppose that a farmer's youngest daughter
Might, as well as the next, unravel
The winding road to Christ's navel.

Who's to know what's knowable?
Milk from the Virgin Mother's breast,
A feather off the Holy Ghost?
The fairy thorn? The holy well?

Our simple wish for there being more to life
Than a job, a car, a house, a wife —
The fixity of running water.

For I like to think, as I step these acres,
That a holy well is no more shallow
Nor plummetless than the pools of Shiloh,
The fairy thorn no less true than the Cross.

III

Mother of our Creator, Mother of our Saviour,
Mother most amiable, Mother most admirable.
Virgin most prudent, Virgin most venerable,
Mother inviolate, Mother undefiled.

And I walk waist-deep among purples and golds
With one arm as long as the other.

Blemish

Were it indeed an accident of birth
That she looks on the gentle earth
And the seemingly gentle sky
Through one brown, and one blue eye.

The Bearded Woman, by Ribera

I've seen one in a fairground,
Swigging a quart of whiskey,
But nothing like this lady
Who squats in the foreground
To suckle the baby,
With what must be her husband
Almost out of the picture.

Might this be the Holy Family
Gone wrong?

Her face belongs to my grand-da
Except that her beard
Is so luxuriantly black.
One pap, her right, is bared
And borrowed by her child,
Who could not be less childlike.
He's ninety, too, if he's a day.

I'm taken completely
By this so unlikely Madonna.

Yet my eye is drawn once again,
Almost against its wishes,
To the figure in the shadows,
Willowy, and clean-shaven,
As if he has simply wandered in
Between mending that fuse
And washing the breakfast dishes.

The Merman

He was ploughing his single furrow
Through the green, heavy sward
Of water. I was sowing winter wheat
At the shoreline, when our farms met.

Not a furrow, quite, I argued.
Nothing would come of his long acre
But breaker growing out of breaker,
The wind-scythe, the rain-harrow.

Had he no wish to own such land
As he might plough round in a day?
What of friendship, love? Such qualities?

He remembered these same fields of corn or hay
When swathes ran high along the ground,
Hearing the cries of one in difficulties.

The Narrow Road to the Deep North

A Japanese soldier
Has just stumbled out of the forest.
The war has been over
These thirty years, and he has lost

All but his ceremonial sword.
We offer him an American cigarette.
He takes it without a word.
For all this comes too late. Too late

To break the sword across his knee,
To be right or wrong.
He means to go back to his old farm

And till the land. Though never to deny
The stone its sling,
The blade of grass its one good arm.

Duffy's Circus

Once Duffy's Circus had shaken out its tent
In the big field near the Moy
God may as well have left Ireland
And gone up a tree. My father had said so.

There was no such thing as the five-legged calf,
The God of Creation
Was the God of Love.
My father chose to share such Nuts of Wisdom.

Yet across the Alps of each other the elephants
Trooped. Nor did it matter
When Wild Bill's Rain Dance
Fell flat. Some clown emptied a bucket of stars

Over the swankiest part of the crowd.
I had lost my father in the rush and slipped
Out the back. Now I heard
For the first time that long-drawn-out cry.

It came from somewhere beyond the corral.
A dwarf on stilts. Another dwarf.
I sidled past some trucks. From under a freighter
I watched a man sawing a woman in half.

Mules

Should they not have the best of both worlds?

Her feet of clay gave the lie
To the star burned in our mare's brow.
Would Parsons' jackass not rest more assured
That cross wrenched from his shoulders?

We had loosed them into one field.
I watched Sam Parsons and my quick father
Tense for the punch below their belts,
For what was neither one thing or the other.

It was as though they had shuddered
To think, of their gaunt, sexless foal
Dropped tonight in the cowshed.

We might yet claim that it sprang from earth
Were it not for the afterbirth
Trailed like some fine, silk parachute,
That we would know from what heights it fell.

from Armageddon, Armageddon

A summer night in Keenaghan
So dark my light had lingered near its lamp
For fear of it. Nor was I less afraid.
At the Mustard Seed Mission all was darkness.

I had gone out with the kettle
To a little stream that lay down in itself
And breathed through a hollow reed
When yon black beetle lighted on my thumb
And tickled along my palm
Like a blood-blister with a mind of its own.

My hand might well have been some flat stone
The way it made for the underside.
I had to turn my wrist against its wont
To have it walk in the paths of uprightness.

Cuba

My eldest sister arrived home that morning
In her white muslin evening dress.
'Who the hell do you think you are,
Running out to dances in next to nothing?
As though we hadn't enough bother
With the world at war, if not at an end.'
My father was pounding the breakfast-table.

'Those Yankees were touch and go as it was –
If you'd heard Patton in Armagh –
But this Kennedy's nearly an Irishman
So he's not much better than ourselves.
And him with only to say the word.
If you've got anything on your mind
Maybe you should make your peace with God.'

I could hear May from beyond the curtain.
'Bless me, Father, for I have sinned.
I told a lie once, I was disobedient once.
And, Father, a boy touched me once.'
'Tell me, child. Was this touch immodest?
Did he touch your breast, for example?'
'He brushed against me, Father. Very gently.'

The Boundary Commission

You remember that village where the border ran
Down the middle of the street,
With the butcher and baker in different states?
Today he remarked how a shower of rain

Had stopped so cleanly across Golightly's lane
It might have been a wall of glass
That had toppled over. He stood there, for ages,
To wonder which side, if any, he should be on.

The Weepies

Most Saturday afternoons
At the local Hippodrome
Saw the Pathe-News rooster,
Then the recurring dream

Of a lonesome drifter
Through uninterrupted range.
Will Hunter, so gifted
He could peel an orange

In a single, fluent gesture,
Was the leader of our gang.
The curtain rose this afternoon
On a lion, not a gong.

When the crippled girl
Who wanted to be a dancer
Met the married man
Who was dying of cancer,

Our hankies unfurled
Like flags of surrender.
I believe something fell asunder
In even Will Hunter's hands.

Immrama

I, too, have trailed my father's spirit
From the mud-walled cabin behind the mountain
Where he was born and bred,
TB and scarlatina,
The farm where he was first hired out,
To Wigan, to Crewe junction,
A building-site from which he disappeared
And took passage, almost, for Argentina.

The mountain is coming down with hazel,
The building-site a slum,
While he has gone no further than Brazil.

That's him on the verandah, drinking rum
With a man who might be a Nazi,
His children asleep under their mosquito-nets.

Lull

I've heard it argued in some quarters
That in Armagh they mow the hay
With only a week to go to Christmas,
That no one's in a hurry

To save it, or their own sweet selves.
Tomorrow is another day,
As your man said on the Mount of Olives.
The same is held of County Derry.

Here and there up and down the country
There are still houses where the fire
Hasn't gone out in a century.

I know that eternal interim;
I think I know what they're waiting for
In Tyrone, Fermanagh, Down and Antrim.

Holy Thursday

They're kindly here, to let us linger so late,
Long after the shutters are up.
A waiter glides from the kitchen with a plate
Of stew, or some thick soup,

And settles himself at the next table but one.
We know, you and I, that it's over,
That something or other has come between
Us, whatever we are, or were.

The waiter swabs his plate with bread
And drains what's left of his wine,
Then rearranges, one by one,
The knife, the fork, the spoon, the napkin,
The table itself, the chair he's simply borrowed,
And smiles, and bows to his own absence.

Truce

It begins with one or two soldiers
And one or two following
With hampers over their shoulders.
They might be off wildfowling

As they would another Christmas Day,
So gingerly they pick their steps.
No one seems sure of what to do.
All stop when one stops.

A fire gets lit. Some spread
Their greatcoats on the frozen ground.
Polish vodka, fruit and bread
Are broken out and passed round.

The air of an old German song,
The rules of Patience, are the secrets
They'll share before long.
They draw on their last cigarettes

As Friday-night lovers, when it's over,
Might get up from their mattresses
To congratulate each other
And exchange names and addresses.

History

Where and when exactly did we first have sex?
Do you remember? Was it Fitzroy Avenue,
Or Cromwell Road, or Notting Hill?
Your place or mine? Marseilles or Aix?
Or as long ago as that Thursday evening
When you and I climbed through the bay window
On the ground floor of Aquinas Hall
And into the room where MacNeice wrote 'Snow',
Or the room where they say he wrote 'Snow'?

Whim

She was sitting with a pint and a small one
That afternoon in the Europa Hotel,
Poring over one of those old legends –
Cu Chulainn and the Birds of Appetite –
When he happened along, and took a pew.

'Pardon me, for I couldn't help but notice
You've got the O'Grady translation.'
'What of it? What's it to you?'
'Standish O'Grady? Very old-fashioned.
Cu Chulainn and the Birds of Appetite?
More like *How Cu Chulainn Got His End*.'
He smiled. She was smiling too.
'If you want the flavour of the original
You should be looking to Kuno Meyer.
As it happens, I've got the very edition
That includes this particular tale.
You could have it on loan, if you like,
If you'd like to call back to my place, now.'

Not that they made it as far as his place.
They would saunter through the Botanic Gardens
Where they held hands, and kissed,
And by and by one thing led to another.
To cut not a very long story short,
Once he got stuck into her he got stuck
Full stop.
          They lay there quietly until dusk
When an attendant found them out.

He called an ambulance, and gently but firmly
They were manhandled on to a stretcher
Like the last of an endangered species.

Ireland

The Volkswagen parked in the gap,
But gently ticking over.
You wonder if it's lovers
And not men hurrying back
Across two fields and a river.

Anseo

When the Master was calling the roll
At the primary school in Collegelands,
You were meant to call back *Anseo*
And raise your hand
As your name occurred.
Anseo, meaning here, here and now,
All present and correct,
Was the first word of Irish I spoke.
The last name on the ledger
Belonged to Joseph Mary Plunkett Ward
And was followed, as often as not,
By silence, knowing looks,
A nod and a wink, the Master's droll
'And where's our little Ward-of-court?'

I remember the first time he came back
The Master had sent him out
Along the hedges
To weigh up for himself and cut
A stick with which he would be beaten.
After a while, nothing was spoken;
He would arrive as a matter of course
With an ash-plant, a salley-rod.
Or, finally, the hazel-wand
He had whittled down to a whip-lash,
Its twist of red and yellow lacquers
Sanded and polished,
And altogether so delicately wrought
That he had engraved his initials on it.

I last met Joseph Mary Plunkett Ward
In a pub just over the Irish border.
He was living in the open,
In a secret camp
On the other side of the mountain.
He was fighting for Ireland,
Making things happen.
And he told me, Joe Ward,
Of how he had risen through the ranks
To Quartermaster, Commandant:
How every morning at parade
His volunteers would call back *Anseo*
And raise their hands
As their names occurred.

Why Brownlee Left

Why Brownlee left, and where he went,
Is a mystery even now.
For if a man should have been content
It was him; two acres of barley,
One of potatoes, four bullocks,
A milker, a slated farmhouse.
He was last seen going out to plough
On a March morning, bright and early.

By noon Brownlee was famous;
They had found all abandoned, with
The last rig unbroken, his pair of black
Horses, like man and wife,
Shifting their weight from foot to
Foot, and gazing into the future.

Promises, Promises

I am stretched out under the lean-to
Of an old tobacco-shed
On a farm in North Carolina.
A cardinal sings from the dogwood
For the love of marijuana.
His song goes over my head.
There is such splendour in the grass
I might be the picture of happiness.
Yet I am utterly bereft
Of the low hills, the open-ended sky,
The wave upon wave of pasture
Rolling in, and just as surely
Falling short of my bare feet.
Whatever is passing is passing me by.

I am with Raleigh, near the Atlantic,
Where we have built a stockade
Around our little colony.
Give him his scallop-shell of quiet,
His staff of faith to walk upon,
His scrip of joy, immortal diet —
We are some eighty souls
On whom Raleigh will hoist his sails.
He will return, years afterwards,
To wonder where and why
We might have altogether disappeared,
Only to glimpse us here and there
As one fair strand in her braid,
The blue in an Indian girl's dead eye.

I am stretched out under the lean-to
Of an old tobacco-shed
On a farm in North Carolina,
When someone or other, warm, naked,
Stirs within my own skeleton
And stands on tip-toe to look out
Over the horizon,
Through the zones, across the ocean.
The cardinal sings from a redbud
For the love of one slender and shy,
The flight after flight of stairs
To her room in Bayswater,
The damson freckle on her throat
That I kissed when we kissed goodbye.

Making the Move

When Ulysses braved the wine-dark sea
He left his bow with Penelope,

Who would bend for no one but himself.
I edge along the book-shelf,

Past bad Lord Byron, Raymond Chandler,
Howard Hughes: The Hidden Years,

Past Blaise Pascal, who, bound in hide,
Divined the void to his left side:

Such books as one may think one owns
Unloose themselves like stones

And clatter down into the wider gulf
Between myself and my good wife;

A primus stove, a sleeping-bag,
The bow I bought through a catalogue

When I was thirteen or fourteen
That would bend, and break, for anyone,

Its boyish length of maple upon maple
Unseasoned and unsupple.

Were I embarking on that wine-dark sea
I would bring my bow along with me.

Immram

I was fairly and squarely behind the eight
That morning in Foster's pool-hall
When it came to me out of the blue
In the shape of a sixteen-ounce billiard cue
That lent what he said some little weight.
'Your old man was an ass-hole.
That makes an ass-hole out of you.'
My grand-father hailed from New York State.
My grand-mother was part Cree.
This must be some new strain in my pedigree.

The billiard-player had been big, and black,
Dressed to kill, or inflict a wound,
And had hung around the pin-table
As long as it took to smoke a panatella.
I was clinging to an ice-pack
On which the Titanic might have foundered
When I was suddenly bedazzled
By a little silver knick-knack
That must have fallen from his hat-band.
I am telling this exactly as it happened.

I suppose that I should have called the cops
Or called it a day and gone home
And done myself, and you, a favour.
But I wanted to know more about my father.
So I drove west to Paradise
Where I was greeted by the distant hum
Of 'Shall We Gather at the River?'
The perfect introduction to the kind of place
Where people go to end their lives.
It might have been 'Bringing In the Sheaves.'

My mother had just been fed by force,
A pint of lukewarm water through a rubber hose.
I hadn't seen her in six months or a year,
Not since my father had disappeared.
Now she'd taken an overdose
Of alcohol and barbiturates,
And this, I learned, was her third.
I was told then by a male nurse
That if I came back at the end of the week
She might be able to bring herself to speak.

Which brought me round to the Atlantic Club.
The Atlantic Club was an old grain-silo
That gave onto the wharf.
Not the kind of place you took your wife
Unless she had it in mind to strip
Or you had a mind to put her up for sale.
I knew how my father had come here by himself
And maybe thrown a little crap
And watched his check double, and treble,
With highball hard on the heels of highball.

She was wearing what looked like a dead fox
Over a low-cut sequinned gown,
And went by the name of Susan, or Suzanne.
A girl who would never pass out of fashion
So long as there's an 'if' in California.
I stood her one or two pink gins
And the talk might have come round to passion
Had it not been for a pair of thugs
Who suggested that we both take a wander,
She upstairs, I into the wild, blue yonder.

They came bearing down on me out of nowhere.
A Buick and a Chevrolet.
They were heading towards a grand slam.
Salami on rye. I was the salami.
So much for my faith in human nature.
The age of chivalry how are you?
But I side-stepped them, neatly as Salome,
So they came up against one another
In a moment of intense heat and light,
Like a couple of turtles on their wedding-night.

Both were dead. Of that I was almost certain.
When I looked into their eyes
I sensed the import of their recent visions,
How you must get all of wisdom
As you pass through a wind-shield.
One's frizzled hair was dyed
A peroxide blond, his sinewy arms emblazoned
With tattoos, his vest marked *Urgent*.
All this was taking on a shape
That might be clearer after a night's sleep.

When the only thing I had ever held in common
With anyone else in the world
Was the ramshackle house on Central Boulevard
That I shared with my child-bride
Until she dropped out to join a commune,
You can imagine how little I was troubled
To kiss goodbye to its weathered clapboard.
When I nudged the rocker on the porch
It rocked as though it might never rest.
It seemed that I would forever be driving west.

I was in luck. She'd woken from her slumbers
And was sitting out among flowering shrubs.
All might have been peace and harmony
In that land of milk and honey
But for the fact that our days are numbered,
But for Foster's, the Atlantic Club,
And now, that my father owed Redpath money.
Redpath. She told me how his empire
Ran a little more than half-way to Hell
But began on the top floor of the Park Hotel.

Steel and glass were held in creative tension
That afternoon in the Park.
I strode through the cavernous lobby
And found myself behind a nervous couple
Who registered as Mr and Mrs Alfred Tennyson.
The unsmiling, balding desk-clerk
Looked like a man who would sell an alibi
To King Kong on the Empire State building,
So I thought better of passing the time of day.
I took the elevator all the way.

You remember how, in a half-remembered dream,
You found yourself in a long corridor,
How behind the first door there was nothing,
Nothing behind the second,
Then how you swayed from room to empty room
Until, beyond that last half-open door
You heard a telephone . . . and you were wakened
By a woman's voice asking you to come
To the Atlantic Club, between six and seven,
And when you came, to come alone.

I was met, not by the face behind the voice,
But by yet another aide-de-camp
Who would have passed for a Barbary pirate
With a line in small-talk like a parrot
And who ferried me past an outer office
To a not ungracious inner sanctum.
I did a breast-stroke through the carpet,
Went under once, only to surface
Alongside the raft of a banquet-table –
A whole roast pig, its mouth fixed on an apple.

Beyond the wall-length, two-way mirror
There was still more to feast your eyes upon
As Susan, or Susannah, danced
Before what looked like an invited audience,
A select band of admirers
To whom she would lay herself open.
I was staring into the middle distance
Where two men and a dog were mowing her meadow
When I was hit by a hypodermic syringe.
And I entered a world equally rich and strange.

There was one who can only have been asleep
Among row upon row of sheeted cadavers
In what might have been the morgue
Of all the cities of America,
Who beckoned me towards her slab
And silently drew back the covers
On the vermilion omega
Where she had been repeatedly stabbed,
Whom I would carry over the threshold of pain
That she might come and come and come again.

I came to, under a steaming pile of trash
In the narrow alley-way
Behind that old Deep Water Baptist mission
Near the corner of Sixteenth and Ocean –
A blue-eyed boy, the Word made flesh
Amid no hosannahs nor hallelujahs
But the strains of Blind Lemon Jefferson
That leaked from the church
Through a hole in a tiny, stained-glass window,
In what was now a torrent, now had dwindled.

And honking to Blind Lemon's blues guitar
Was a solitary, black cat
Who would have turned the heads of Harlem.
He was no louder than a fire-alarm,
A full-length coat of alligator,
An ermine stole, his wide-brimmed hat
Festooned with family heirlooms.
I watch him trickle a fine, white powder
Into his palm, so not a grain would spill,
Then snort it through a rolled-up dollar bill.

This was angel dust, dust from an angel's wing
Where it glanced off the land of cocaine,
Be that Bolivia, Peru,
Or snow from the slopes of the Andes, so pure
It would never melt in spring.
But you know how over every Caliban
There's Ariel, and behind him, Prospero;
Everyone taking a cut, dividing and conquering
With lactose and dextrose,
Everyone getting right up everyone else's nose.

I would tiptoe round by the side of the church
For a better view. Some fresh cement.
I trod as lightly there
As a mere mortal at Grauman's Chinese Theatre.
An oxyacetylene torch.
There were two false-bottomed
Station-wagons. I watched Mr See-You-Later
Unload a dozen polythene packs
From one to the other. *The Urgent Shipping Company.*
It behoved me to talk to the local P.D.

'My father, God rest him, he held this theory
That the Irish, the American Irish,
Were really the thirteenth tribe,
The Israelites of Europe.
All along, my father believed in fairies
But he might as well have been Jewish.'
His laugh was a slight hiccup.
I guessed that Lieutenant Brendan O'Leary's
Grandmother's pee was green,
And that was why she had to leave old Skibbereen.

Now, what was all this about the Atlantic cabaret,
Urgent, the top floor of the Park?
When had I taken it into my head
That somebody somewhere wanted to see me dead?
Who? No, Redpath was strictly on the level.
So why, rather than drag in the Narcs,
Why didn't he and I drive over to Ocean Boulevard
At Eighteenth Street, or wherever?
Would I mind stepping outside while he made a call
To such-and-such a luminary at City Hall?

We counted thirty-odd of those brown-eyed girls
Who ought to be in pictures,
Bronzed, bleached, bare-breasted,
Bare-assed to a man,
All sitting, cross-legged, in a circle
At the feet of this life-guard out of Big Sur
Who made an exhibition
Of his dorsals and his pectorals
While one by one his disciples took up the chant
The Lord is my surf-board. I shall not want.

He went on to explain to O'Leary and myself
How only that morning he had acquired the lease
On the old Baptist mission,
Though his was a wholly new religion.
He called it *The Way of the One Wave.*
This one wave was sky-high, like a wall of glass,
And had come to him in a vision.
You could ride it forever, effortlessly.
The Lieutenant was squatting before his new guru.
I would inform the Missing Persons Bureau.

His name? I already told you his name.
Forty-nine. Fifty come July.
Five ten or eleven. One hundred and eighty pounds.
He could be almost anyone.
And only now was it brought home to me
How rarely I looked in his eyes,
Which were hazel. His hair was mahogany brown.
There was a scar on his left forearm
From that time he got himself caught in the works
Of a saw-mill near Ithaca, New York.

I was just about getting things into perspective
When a mile-long white Cadillac
Came sweeeeping out of the distant past
Like a wayward Bay mist,
A transport of joy. There was the chauffeur
From the 1931 Sears Roebuck catalogue,
Susannah, as you guessed,
And this refugee from F. Scott Fitzgerald
Who looked as if he might indeed own the world.
His name was James Earl Caulfield III.

This was how it was. My father had been a mule.
He had flown down to Rio
Time and time again. But he courted disaster.
He tried to smuggle a wooden statue
Through the airport at Lima.
The Christ of the Andes. The statue was hollow.
He stumbled. It went and shattered.
And he had to stand idly by
As a cool fifty or sixty thousand dollars' worth
Was trampled back into the good earth.

He would flee, to La Paz, then to Buenos Aires,
From alias to alias.
I imagined him sitting outside a hacienda
Somewhere in the Argentine.
He would peer for hours
Into the vastness of the pampas.
Or he might be pointing out the constellations
Of the Southern hemisphere
To the open-mouthed child at his elbow.
He sleeps with a loaded pistol under his pillow.

The mile-long white Cadillac had now wrapped
Itself round the Park Hotel.
We were spirited to the nineteenth floor
Where Caulfield located a secret door.
We climbed two perilous flights of steps
To the exclusive penthouse suite.
A moment later I was ushered
Into a chamber sealed with black drapes.
As I grew accustomed to the gloom
I realized there was someone else in the room.

He was huddled on an old orthopaedic mattress,
The makings of a skeleton,
Naked but for a pair of draw-string shorts.
His hair was waistlength, as was his beard.
He was covered in bedsores.
He raised one talon.
'I forgive you,' he croaked. 'And I forget.
On your way out, you tell that bastard
To bring me a dish of ice-cream.
I want Baskin-Robbins banana-nut ice-cream.'

I shimmied about the cavernous lobby.
Mr and Mrs Alfred Tennyson
Were ahead of me through the revolving door.
She tipped the bell-hop five dollars.
There was a steady stream of people
That flowed in one direction,
Faster and deeper,
That I would go along with, happily,
As I made my way back, like any other pilgrim,
To Main Street, to Foster's pool-room.

Trance

My mother opens the scullery door
On Christmas Eve, 1954,
to empty the dregs
of the teapot on the snowy flags.
A wind out of Siberia
carries such voices as will carry
through to the kitchen —

Someone mutters a flame from lichen
and eats the red-and-white Fly Agaric
while the others hunker in the dark,
taking it in turn
to drink his mind-expanding urine.
One by one their reindeer
nuzzle in.

My mother slams the door
on her star-cluster of dregs
and packs me off to bed.
At 2 a.m. I will clamber downstairs
to glimpse the red-and-white
up the chimney, my new rocking-horse
as yet unsteady on its legs.

Yggdrasill

From below, the waist-thick pine
seemed to arch
its back. It is a birch,
perhaps. At any rate, I could discern
a slight curvature of the spine.

They were gathered in knots
to watch me go.
A pony fouled the hard-packed snow
with her glib cairn,
someone opened a can of apricots.

As I climb
my nose is pressed to the bark.
The mark
of a cigarette burn
from your last night with him.

A snapshot of you and your sister
walking straight
through 1958,
The Works of Laurence Sterne
your only aid to posture.

The air is aerosol-
blue and chill. I have notched
up your pitch-
pine scent and the maidenhair fern's
spry arousal.

And it would be just swell and dandy
to answer
them with my tonsure,
to return
with the black page from *Tristram Shandy*.

Yet the lichened
tree trunk will taper
to a point where one scrap of paper
is spiked, and my people yearn
for a legend:

It may not be today
or tomorrow, but sooner or later
the Russians will water
their horses on the shores of Lough Erne
and Lough Neagh.

Gathering Mushrooms

The rain comes flapping through the yard
like a tablecloth that she hand-embroidered.
My mother has left it on the line.
It is sodden with rain.
The mushroom shed is windowless, wide,
its high-stacked wooden trays
hosed down with formaldehyde.
And my father has opened the Gates of Troy
to that first load of horse manure.
Barley straw. Gypsum. Dried blood. Ammonia.
Wagon after wagon
blusters in, a self-renewing gold-black dragon
we push to the back of the mind.
We have taken our pitchforks to the wind.

All brought back to me that September evening
fifteen years on. The pair of us
tripping through Barnett's fair demesne
like girls in long dresses
after a hail-storm.
We might have been thinking of the fire-bomb
that sent Malone House sky-high
and its priceless collection of linen
sky-high.
We might have wept with Elizabeth McCrum.
We were thinking only of psilocybin.
You sang of the maid you met on the dewy grass —
*And she stooped so low gave me to know
it was mushrooms she was gathering O.*

He'll be wearing that same old donkey-jacket
and the sawn-off waders.
He carries a knife, two punnets, a bucket.
He reaches far into his own shadow.
We'll have taken him unawares
and stand behind him, slightly to one side.
He is one of those ancient warriors
before the rising tide.
He'll glance back from under his peaked cap
without breaking rhythm:
his coaxing a mushroom — a flat or a cup —
the nick against his right thumb;
the bucket then, the punnet to left or right,
and so on and so forth till kingdom come.

We followed the overgrown towpath by the Lagan.
The sunset would deepen through cinnamon
to aubergine,
the wood-pigeon's concerto for oboe and strings,
allegro, blowing your mind.
And you were suddenly out of my ken, hurtling
towards the ever-receding ground,
into the maw
of a shimmering green-gold dragon.
You discovered yourself in some outbuilding
with your long-lost companion, me,
though my head had grown into the head of a horse
that shook its dirty-fair mane
and spoke this verse:

Come back to us. However cold and raw, your feet
were always meant
to negotiate terms with bare cement.
Beyond this concrete wall is a wall of concrete
and barbed wire. Your only hope
is to come back. If sing you must, let your song
tell of treading your own dung,
let straw and dung give a spring to your step.
If we never live to see the day we leap
into our true domain,
lie down with us now and wrap
yourself in the soiled grey blanket of Irish rain
that will, one day, bleach itself white.
Lie down with us and wait.

The Right Arm

I was three-ish
when I plunged my arm into the sweet-jar
for the last bit of clove-rock.

We kept a shop in Eglish
that sold bread, milk, butter, cheese,
bacon and eggs,
Andrews Liver Salts,
and, until now, clove-rock.

I would give my right arm to have known then
how Eglish was itself wedged between
ecclesia and *église*.

The Eglish sky was its own stained-glass vault
and my right arm was sleeved in glass
that has yet to shatter.

The Sightseers

My father and mother, my brother and sister
and I, with uncle Pat, our dour best-loved uncle,
had set out that Sunday afternoon in July
in his broken-down Ford

not to visit some graveyard — one died of shingles,
one of fever, another's knees turned to jelly —
but the brand-new roundabout at Ballygawley,
the first in mid-Ulster.

Uncle Pat was telling us how the B-Specials
had stopped him one night somewhere near Ballygawley
and smashed his bicycle

and made him sing the Sash and curse the Pope of Rome.
They held a pistol so hard against his forehead
there was still the mark of an O when he got home.

Quoof

How often have I carried our family word
for the hot water bottle
to a strange bed,
as my father would juggle a red-hot half-brick
in an old sock
to his childhood settle.
I have taken it into so many lovely heads
or laid it between us like a sword.

An hotel room in New York City
with a girl who spoke hardly any English,
my hand on her breast
like the smouldering one-off spoor of the yeti
or some other shy beast
that has yet to enter the language.

Cherish the Ladies

In this, my last poem about my father,
there may be time enough
for him to fill their drinking-trough
and run his eye over

his three mooley heifers.
Such a well-worn path,
I know, from here to the galvanized bath.
I know, too, you would rather

I saw behind the hedge to where the pride
of the herd, though not an Irish
bull, would cherish
the ladies with his electric cattle-prod.

As it is, in my last poem about my father
he opens the stand-pipe
and the water scurries along the hose
till it's curled

in the bath. One heifer
may look up
and make a mental note, then put her nose
back to the salt-lick of the world.

Mink

A mink escaped from a mink-farm
in South Armagh
is led to the grave of Robert Nairac
by the fur-lined hood of his anorak.

The Frog

Comes to mind as another small upheaval
amongst the rubble.
His eye matches exactly the bubble
in my spirit-level.
I set aside hammer and chisel
and take him on the trowel.

The entire population of Ireland
springs from a pair left to stand
overnight in a pond
in the gardens of Trinity College,
two bottles of wine left there to chill
after the Act of Union.

There is, surely, in this story
a moral. A moral for our times.
What if I·put him to my head
and squeezed it out of him,
like the juice of freshly squeezed limes,
or a lemon sorbet?

The Unicorn Defends Himself

Somewhere in or around the turn
of the sixteenth century,
we come upon the fourth
in a series of Flemish tapestries
on the hunt of the unicorn.

Kicking out with his tattered hind
hooves, he tilts
at a hunting-hound
with his barley-sugar stick of horn;
the unicorn defends himself.

II

Once you swallowed a radar-blip
of peyote
you were out of your tree,
you hadn't a baldy
where you were or who you were with.

Only that you had fallen asleep
on the water bed
in a loft on the Lower East Side,
and woke between two bodies, true,
one wire-haired and one smooth.

The focal point is not, in truth,
his *coup de ventre*
to the milt-
sleek hunting-hound,
by which our eye is led astray.

Everything centres
on that spear tip poised to squander
the cleft
of his 'innocent behind'.
At Houston Street and Lafayette

the unicorn defends himself.

Aisling

I was making my way home late one night
this summer, when I staggered
into a snow drift.

Her eyes spoke of a sloe-year,
her mouth a year of haws.

Was she Aurora, or the goddess Flora,
Artemidora, or Venus bright,
or Anorexia, who left
a lemon stain on my flannel sheet?

It's all much of a muchness.

In Belfast's Royal Victoria Hospital
a kidney machine
supports the latest hunger-striker
to have called off his fast, a saline
drip into his bag of brine.

A lick and a promise. Cuckoo spittle.
I hand my sample to Doctor Maw.
She gives me back a confident *All Clear*.

The More a Man Has the More a Man Wants

At four in the morning he wakes
to the yawn of brakes,
the snore of a diesel engine.
Gone. All she left
is a froth of bra and panties.
The scum of the Seine
and the Farset.
Gallogly squats in his own pelt.
A sodium street light
has brought a new dimension
to their black taxi.
By the time they force an entry
he'll have skedaddled
among hen runs and pigeon lofts.

The charter flight from Florida
touched down at Aldergrove
minutes earlier,
at 3.54 a.m.
Its excess baggage takes the form
of Mangas Jones, Esquire,
who is, as it turns out, Apache.
He carries only hand luggage.
'Anything to declare?'
He opens the powder-blue attaché-
case. 'A pebble of quartz.'
'You're an Apache?' 'Mescalero.'
He follows the corridor's
arroyo till the signs read *Hertz*.

He is going to put his foot down
on a patch of waste ground
along the Stranmillis embankment
when he gets wind
of their impromptu fire.
The air above the once-sweet stream
is aquarium-
drained.
And six, maybe seven, skinheads
have formed a quorum
round a burnt-out heavy-duty tyre.
So intent on sniffing glue
they may not notice Gallogly,
or, if they do, are so far gone.

Three miles west as the crow flies
an all-night carry-out
provides the cover
for an illegal drinking club.
While the bar man unpacks a crate
of Coca-Cola,
one cool customer
takes on all comers in a video game.
He grasps what his two acolytes
have failed to seize.
Don't they know what kind of take-away
this is, the glipes?
Vietmanese. Viet-ma-friggin'-*knees*.
He drops his payload of napalm.

Gallogly is wearing a candy-stripe
king-size sheet,
a little something he picked up
off a clothes line.
He is driving a milk van
he borrowed from the Belfast Co-op
while the milkman's back
was turned.
He had given the milkman a playful
rabbit punch.
When he stepped on the gas
he flooded the street
with broken glass.
He is trying to keep a low profile.

The unmarked police car draws level
with his last address.
A sergeant and eight constables
pile out of a tender
and hammer up the stairs.
The street bristles with static.
Their sniffer dog, a Labrador bitch,
bursts into the attic
like David Balfour in *Kidnapped*.
A constable on his first dawn swoop
leans on a shovel.
He has turned over a
new leaf in her ladyship's herb patch.
They'll take it back for analysis.

All a bit much after the night shift
to meet a milkman
who's double-parked his van
closing your front door after him.
He's sporting your
Donegal tweed suit and your
Sunday shoes and politely raises your
hat as he goes by.
You stand there with your mouth open
as he climbs into the still-warm
driving seat of your Cortina
and screeches off towards the motorway,
leaving you uncertain
of your still-warm wife's damp tuft.

Someone on their way to early Mass
will find her hog-tied
to the chapel gates –
O Child of Prague –
big-eyed, anorexic.
The lesson for today
is pinned to her bomber jacket.
It seems to read *Keep off the Grass*.
Her lovely head has been chopped
and changed.
For Beatrice, whose fathers
knew Louis Quinze,
to have come to this, her perruque
of tar and feathers.

He is pushing the maroon Cortina
through the sedge
on the banks of the Callan.
It took him a mere forty minutes
to skite up the M1.
He followed the exit sign
for Loughgall and hared
among the top-heavy apple orchards.
This stretch of the Armagh/Tyrone
border was planted by Warwickshiremen
who planted in turn
their familiar quick-set damson hedges.
The Cortina goes to the bottom.
Gallogly swallows a plummy-plum-plum.

'I'll warrant them's the very pair
o' boys I seen abroad
in McParland's bottom, though where
in under God —
for thou art so possessed with murd'rous hate —
where they come from God only knows.'
'They were mad for a bite o' mate,
I s'pose.'
'I doubt so. I come across a brave dale
o' half-chawed damsels. Wanst wun disappeared
I follied the wun as yelly as Indy male.'
'Ye weren't afeared?'
'I follied him.' 'God save us.'
'An' he driv away in a van belongin' t'*Avis*.'

The grass sprightly as Astroturf
in the September frost
and a mist
here where the ground is low.
He seizes his own wrist
as if, as if
Blind Pew again seized Jim
at the sign of the 'Admiral Benbow'.
As if Jim Hawkins led Blind Pew
to Billy Bones
and they were all one and the same,
he stares in disbelief
at an Aspirin-white spot he pressed
into his own palm.

Gallogly's thorn-proof tweed jacket
is now several sizes too big.
He has flopped
down in a hay shed
to ram a wad of hay into the toe
of each of his ill-fitting
brogues, when he gets the drift
of ham and eggs.
Now he's led by his own wet nose
to the hacienda-style
farmhouse, a baggy-kneed animated
bear drawn out of the woods
by an apple pie
left to cool on a windowsill.

She was standing at the picture window
with a glass of water
and a Valium
when she caught your man
in the reflection of her face.
He came
shaping past the milking parlour
as if he owned the place.
Such is the integrity
of their quarrel
that she immediately took down
the legally held shotgun
and let him have both barrels.
She had wanted only to clear the air.

Half a mile away across the valley
her husband's U.D.R. patrol
is mounting a check-point.
He pricks up his ears
at the crack
of her prematurely arthritic hip-
joint,
and commandeers one of the jeeps.
There now, only a powder burn
as if her mascara had run.
The bloody puddle
in the yard, and the shilly-shally
of blood like a command wire
petering out behind a milk churn.

A hole in the heart, an ovarian
cyst.
Coming up the Bann
in a bubble.
Disappearing up his own bum.
Or, running on the spot
with all the minor aplomb
of a trick-cyclist.
So thin, side-on, you could spit
through him.
His six foot of pump water
bent double
in agony or laughter.
Keeping down-wind of everything.

White Annetts. Gillyflowers. Angel Bites.
When he names the forgotten names
of apples
he has them all off pat.
His eye like the eye of a travelling rat
lights on the studied negligence
of these scraws of turf.
A tarpaulin. A waterlogged pit.
He will take stock of the Kalashnikov's
filed-down serial number,
seven sticks of unstable
commercial gelignite
that have already begun to weep.
Red Strokes. Sugar Sweet. Widows Whelps.

Buy him a drink and he'll regale you
with how he came in for a cure
one morning after the night before
to the *Las Vegas* Lounge and Cabaret.
He was crossing the bar's
eternity of parquet floor
when his eagle eye
saw something move on the horizon.
If it wasn't an Indian.
A Sioux. An ugly Sioux.
He means, of course, an Oglala
Sioux busily tracing the family tree
of an Ulsterman who had some hand
in the massacre at Wounded Knee.

He will answer the hedge-sparrow's
Littlebitofbreadandnocheese
with a whole bunch
of freshly picked watercress,
a bulb of garlic,
sorrel,
with many-faceted blackberries.
Gallogly is out to lunch.
When his cock rattles its sabre
he takes it in his dab
hand, plants one chaste kiss
on its forelock,
and then, with a birl and a skirl,
tosses it off like a caber.

The U.D.R. corporal had come off duty
to be with his wife
while the others set about
a follow-up search.
When he tramped out just before twelve
to exercise the greyhound
he was hit by a single high-velocity
shot.
You could, if you like, put your fist
in the exit wound
in his chest.
He slumps
in the spume of his own arterial blood
like an overturned paraffin lamp.

Gallogly lies down in the sheugh
to munch
through a Beauty of
Bath. He repeats himself, *Bath*,
under his garlic-breath.
Sheugh, he says, *Sheugh*.
He is finding that first 'sh'
increasingly difficult to manage.
Sh-leeps. A milkmaid sinks
her bare foot
to the ankle
in a simmering dung hill
and fills the slot
with beastlings for him to drink.

[89]

In Ovid's conspicuously tongue-in-cheek
account of an eyeball
to eyeball
between the goddess Leto
and a shower of Lycian reed cutters
who refuse her a cup of cloudy
water
from their churned-up lake,
Live then forever in that lake of yours,
she cries, and has them
bubble
and squeak
and plonk themselves down as bullfrogs
in their icy jissom.

A country man kneels on his cap
beside his neighbour's fresh
grave-mud
as Gallogly kneels to lap
the primrose-yellow
custard.
The knees of his hand-me-down duds
are gingerish.
A pernickety seven-
year-old girl-child
parades in her mother's trousseau
and mumbles a primrose
Kleenex tissue
to make sure her lipstick's even.

Gallogly has only to part the veil
of its stomach wall
to get right under the skin,
the spluttering heart
and collapsed lung,
of the horse in *Guernica*.
He flees the Museum of Modern Art
with its bit between his teeth.
When he began to cough
blood, Hamsun rode the Minneapolis
New York night train
on top of the dining-car.
One long, inward howl.
A porter-drinker without a thrapple.

A weekend trip to the mountains
North of Boston
with Alice, Alice A.
and her paprika hair,
the ignition key
to her family's Winnebago camper,
her quim
biting the leg off her.
In the oyster bar
of Grand Central Station
she gobbles a dozen Chesapeakes –
'Oh, I'm not particular as to size' –
and, with a flourish of tabasco,
turns to gobble him.

A brewery lorry on a routine delivery
is taking a slow,
dangerous bend.
The driver's blethering
his code name
over the Citizens' Band
when someone ambles
in front of him. Go, Johnny, Go, Go, Go.
He's been dry-gulched
by a sixteen-year-old numb
with Mogadon,
whose face is masked by the seamless
black stocking filched
from his mum.

When who should walk in but Beatrice,
large as life, or larger,
sipping her one glass of lager
and singing her one song.
If he had it to do all over again
he would let her shave his head
in memory of '98
and her own, the French, Revolution.
The son of the King of the Moy
met this child on the Roxborough
estate. *Noblesse*, she said. *Noblesse
oblige*. And her tiny nipples
were bruise-bluish, wild raspberries.
The song she sang was 'The Croppy Boy'.

Her *grand'mère* was once asked to tea
by Gertrude Stein,
and her *grand'mère* and Gertrude
and Alice B., *chère* Alice B.
with her hook-nose,
the three of them sat in the nude
round the petits fours
and repeated *Eros is Eros is Eros*.
If he had it to do all over again
he would still be taken in
by her Alice B. Toklas
Nameless Cookies
and those new words she had him learn:
hash, hashish, *lo perfido assassin*.

Once the local councillor straps
himself into the safety belt
of his Citroën
and skids up the ramp
from the municipal car park
he upsets the delicate balance
of a mercury-tilt
boobytrap.
Once they collect his smithereens
he doesn't quite add up.
They're shy of a foot, and a calf
which stems
from his left shoe like a severely
pruned-back shrub.

Ten years before. The smooth-as-a-
front-lawn at Queen's
where she squats
before a psilocybin god.
The indomitable gentle-bush
that had Lanyon or Lynn
revise their elegant ground plan
for the university quad.
With calmness, with care,
with breast milk, with dew.
There's no cure now.
There's nothing left to do.
The mushrooms speak through her.
Hush-hush.

'Oh, I'm not particular as to size,'
Alice hastily replied
and broke off a bit of the edge
with each hand
and set to work very carefully,
nibbling
first at one
and then the other.
On the Staten Island Ferry
two men are dickering
over the price
of a shipment of Armalites,
as Henry Thoreau was wont to quibble
with Ralph Waldo Emerson.

That last night in the Algonquin
he met with a flurry
of sprites,
the assorted shades
of Wolfe Tone, Napper Tandy,
a sanguine
Michael Cusack
brandishing his blackthorn.
Then, Thomas Meagher
darts up from the Missouri
on a ray
of the morning star
to fiercely ask
what has become of Irish hurling.

Everyone has heard the story of
a strong and beautiful bug
which came out of the dry leaf
of an old table of apple-tree wood
that stood
in a farmer's kitchen in Massachusetts
and which was heard gnawing out
for several weeks –
When the phone trills
he is careful not to lose his page –
Who knows what beautiful and winged life
whose egg
has been buried for ages
may unexpectedly come forth? 'Tell-tale.'

Gallogly carries a hunting bow
equipped
with a bow sight
and a quiver
of hunting arrows
belonging to her brother.
Alice has gone a little way off
to do her job.
A timber wolf,
a caribou,
or merely a trick of the light?
As, listlessly,
he lobs
an arrow into the undergrowth.

Had you followed the river Callan's
Pelorus Jack
through the worst drought
in living memory
to the rains of early Autumn
when it scrubs its swollen,
scab-encrusted back
under a bridge, the bridge you look down from,
you would be unlikely to pay much heed
to yet another old banger
no one could be bothered to tax,
or a beat-up fridge
well-stocked with gelignite,
or some five hundred yards of Cortex.

He lopes after the dribs of blood
through the pine forest
till they stop dead
in the ruins of a longhouse
or hogan.
Somehow, he finds his way
back to their tent.
Not so much as a whiff of her musk.
The girl behind the Aer Lingus
check-in desk
at Logan
is wearing the same scent
and an embroidered capital letter *A*
on her breast.

Was she Aurora, or the goddess Flora,
Artemidora, or Venus bright,
or Helen fair beyond compare
that Priam stole from the Grecian sight?
Quite modestly she answered me
and she gave her head one fetch up
and she said I am gathering musheroons
to make my mammy ketchup.
The dunt and dunder
of a culvert-bomb
wakes him
as it might have woke Leander.
And she said I am gathering musheroons
to make my mammy ketchup O.

Predictable as the gift of the gab
or a drop of the craythur
he noses round the six foot deep
crater.
Oblivious to their Landrover's
olive-drab
and the Burgundy berets
of a snatch-squad of Paratroopers.
Gallogly, or Gollogly,
otherwise known as Golightly,
otherwise known as Ingoldsby,
otherwise known as English,
gives forth one low cry of anguish
and agrees to come quietly.

They have bundled him into the cell
for a strip-
search.
He perches
on the balls of his toes, my my,
with his legs spread
till both his instep arches
fall.
He holds himself at arm's
length from the brilliantly Snowcem-ed
wall, a game bird
hung by its pinion tips
till it drops, in the fullness of time,
from the mast its colours are nailed to.

They have left him to cool his heels
after the obligatory
bath,
the mug shots, fingerprints
et cetera.
He plumps the thin bolster
and hints
at the slop bucket.
Six o'clock.
From the A Wing of Armagh jail
he can make out
the Angelus bell
of St Patrick's cathedral
and a chorus of 'For God and Ulster'.

The brewery lorry's stood at a list
by the *Las Vegas*
throughout the afternoon,
its off-side rear tyres down.
As yet, no one has looked agog
at the smuts and rusts
of a girlie mag
in disarray on the passenger seat.
An almost invisible, taut
fishing line
runs from the Playmate's navel
to a pivotal
beer keg.
As yet, no one has risen to the bait.

I saw no mountains, no enormous spaces,
no magical growth and metamorphosis
of buildings, nothing remotely like
a drama or a parable
in which he dons these lime-green
dungarees,
green Wellingtons,
a green helmet of aspect terrible.
The other world to which mescalin
admitted me was not the world of visions;
it existed out there, in what I could see
with my eyes open.
He straps a chemical pack on his back
and goes in search of some Gawain.

Gallogly pads along the block
to raise his visor
at the first peep-hole.
He shamelessly
takes in her lean piglet's
back, the back
and boyish hams
of a girl at stool.
At last. A tiny goat's-pill.
A stub of crayon
with which she has squiggled
a shamrock, yes,
but a shamrock after the school
of Pollock, Jackson Pollock.

I stopped and stared at her face to face
and on the spot a name came to me,
a name with a smooth, nervous sound:
Ylayali.
When she was very close
I drew myself up straight
and said in an impressive voice,
'Miss, you are losing your book.'
And Beatrice, for it is she, she squints
through the spy-hole
to pass him an orange,
an Outspan orange some visitor has spiked
with a syringe-ful
of vodka.

The more a man has the more a man wants,
the same I don't think true.
For I never met a man with one black eye
who ever wanted two.
In the *Las Vegas* Lounge and Cabaret
the resident group —
pot bellies, Aran knits —
have you eating out of their hands.
Never throw a brick at a drowning man
when you're near to a grocer's store.
Just throw him a cake of Sunlight soap,
let him wash himself ashore.
You will act the galoot, and gallivant,
and call for another encore.

Gallogly, Gallogly, O Gallogly
juggles
his name like an orange
between his outsize baseball glove
paws,
and ogles
a moon that's just out of range
beyond the perimeter wall.
He works a gobbet of Brylcreem
into his quiff
and delves
through sand and gravel,
shrugging it off
his velveteen shoulders and arms.

> *Just*
> *throw*
> *him*
> *a*
> *cake*
> *of*
> *Sunlight*
> *soap,*
> *let*
> *him*
> *wash*
> *him-*
> *self*
> *ashore.*

Into a picture by Edward Hopper
of a gas station
in the mid-West
where Hopper takes at his theme
light, the spooky
glow of an illuminated sign
reading Esso or Mobil
or what-have-you—
into such a desolate oval
ride two youths on a motorbike.
A hand gun. Balaclavas.
The pump attendant's grown so used
to hold-ups he calls after them:
Beannacht Dé ar an obair.

The pump attendant's not to know
he's being watched by a gallowglass
hot-foot from a woodcut
by Derricke,
who skips across the forecourt
and kicks the black
plastic bucket
they left as a memento.
Nor is the gallowglass any the wiser.
The bucket's packed with fertilizer
and a heady brew
of sugar and Paraquat's
relentlessly gnawing its way through
the floppy knot of a Durex.

It was this self-same pump attendant
who dragged the head and torso
clear
and mouthed an Act of Contrition
in the frazzled ear
and overheard
those already-famous last words
Moose . . . Indian.
'Next of all wus the han'.' 'Be Japers.'
'The sodgers cordonned-off the area
wi' what-ye-may-call-it tape.'
'Lunimous.' 'They foun' this hairy
han' wi' a drowneded man's grip
on a lunimous stone no bigger than a . . .'

'Huh.'

Bears

I ought to begin with Evelyn Waugh's
'How old's that noise?'

when you wander arbi-
trarily into *Le Déjeuner sur l'herbe*.

Wahl, Wahl, Wahl,
your great-great-grandmother's wail

who froze to death in a cranberry-patch
among the Pennsylvania Dutch.

*

Yaddo. Your father consecrating priests
while Lowell and Roethke
made like bears and beasts.

*

I can no more calm your dutiful outcry
than the luncheon-guest
who dutifully clasps you to his breast.

The Ox

They had driven for three hours non-stop
that April afternoon
to see the Burren's orchids
in bloom.

Milltown Malbay. They parked
in front of a butcher's shop.
'A month too early. I might have known.'
'Let's find a room.'

They reversed away from the window.
To the right hung
one ox-tail,

to the left one ox-tongue.
'What's the matter? What's got into you?'
'Absolutely nothing at all.'

The Main-Mast

Next morning two huskies
lie at the foot
of our bed
in a death-embrace.

Half-dog, half-wolf.
They've polished off
their harness,
rivets and all,

and made short work
of your coat
and boots.
Your matching luggage

you've bundled
into a cabin
on the *Alhambra*, whose
captain will chop down

and burn his
main-mast for a head of steam,
then limp into New York
in record time.

The Lass of Aughrim

On a tributary of the Amazon
and Indian boy
steps out of the forest
and strikes up on a flute.

Imagine my delight
when we cut the outboard motor
and I recognize the strains
of *The Lass of Aughrim.*

'He hopes,' Jesus explains,
'to charm
fish from the water

on what was the tibia
of a priest
from a long-abandoned Mission.'

The Marriage of Strongbow and Aoife

I might as well be another guest
at the wedding-feast
of Strongbow and Aoife Mac Murrough
as watch you, Mary,

try to get to grips
with a spider-crab's
crossbow and cuirass.
A creative pause before the second course

of Ireland's whole ox on a spit;
the invisible waitress
brings us each a Calvados and water-ice.

It is as if someone had slipped
a double-edged knife between my ribs
and hit the spot exactly.

The Wishbone

Maureen in England, Joseph in Guelph,
my mother in her grave.

*

At three o'clock in the afternoon
we watch the Queen's
message to the Commonwealth
with the sound turned off.

*

He seems to favour *Camelot*
over *To Have And Have Not.*

*

Yet we agree, my father and myself,
that here is more than enough
for two; a frozen chicken,
spuds, sprouts, Paxo sage and onion.

*

The wishbone like a rowelled spur
on the fibula of Sir— or Sir—.

The Mist-Net

Though he checked the mist-net
every day for a month

he caught only two tiny birds,
one Pernod-sip,

one tremulous crème-de-menthe:
their tiny sobs

were his mother's dying words;
You mustn't. You mustn't.

Meeting the British

We met the British in the dead of winter.
The sky was lavender

and the snow lavender-blue.
I could hear, far below,

the sound of two streams coming together
(both were frozen over)

and, no less strange,
myself calling out in French

across that forest-
clearing. Neither General Jeffrey Amherst

nor Colonel Henry Bouquet
could stomach our willow-tobacco.

As for the unusual
scent when the Colonel shook out his hand-

kerchief: *C'est la lavande,*
une fleur mauve comme le ciel.

They gave us six fishhooks
and two blankets embroidered with smallpox.

Ontario

I spent last night in the nursery of a house in Pennsylvania. When I put out the light I made my way, barefoot, through the aftermath of Brandywine Creek. The constellations of the northern hemisphere were picked out in luminous paint on the ceiling. I lay under a comforting, phosphorescent Plough, thinking about where the Plough stopped being the Plough and became the Big Dipper. About the astronomer I met in Philadelphia who had found a star with a radio telescope. The star is now named after her, whatever her name happens to be. As all these stars grew dim, it seemed like a good time to rerun my own dream-visions. They had flashed up just as I got into bed on three successive nights in 1972. The first was a close-up of a face, Cox's face, falling. I heard next morning how he had come home drunk and taken a nose-dive down the stairs. Next, my uncle Pat's face, falling in slo-mo like the first, but bloody. It turned out he had slipped off a ladder on a building-site. His forehead needed seven stitches. Lastly, a freeze-frame trickle of water or glycerine on a sheet of smoked glass or perspex. I see it in shaving-mirrors. Dry Martinis. Women's tears. On windshields. As planes take off or land. I remembered how I was meant to fly to Toronto this morning, to visit my younger brother. He used to be a research assistant at the University of Guelph, where he wrote a thesis on nitrogen-fixing in soya beans, or symbiosis, or some such mystery. He now works for the Corn Producers' Association of Ontario. On my last trip we went to a disco in the Park Plaza, where I helped a girl in a bin-liner dress to find her contact-lens.

– Did you know that Spinoza was a lens-grinder?
– Are you for real?

Joe was somewhere in the background, sniggering, flicking cosmic dandruff from his shoulders.

– A lens, I went on, is really a lentil. A pulse.

Her back was an imponderable, green furrow in the ultra-violet strobe.

– Did *you* know that Yonge Street's the longest street in the world?

– I can't say that I did.

– Well, it starts a thousand miles to the north, and it ends right here.

The Coney

Although I have never learned to mow
I suddenly found myself half-way through
last year's pea-sticks
and cauliflower-stalks
in our half-acre of garden.
My father had always left the whetstone
safely wrapped
in his old, tweed cap
and balanced on one particular plank
beside the septic tank.

This past winter he had been too ill
to work. The scythe would dull
so much more quickly in my hands
than his, and was so often honed,
that while the blade
grew less and less a blade
the whetstone had entirely disappeared
and a lop-eared
coney was now curled inside the cap.
He whistled to me through the gap

in his front teeth;
'I was wondering, chief,
if you happen to know the name
of the cauliflowers in your cold-frame
that you still hope to dibble
in this unenviable
bit of ground?'
'They would be *All the Year Round*.'
'I guessed as much'; with that he swaggered
along the diving-board

and jumped. The moment he hit the water
he lost his tattered
bathing-togs
to the swimming-pool's pack of dogs.
'Come in'; this flayed
coney would parade
and pirouette like honey on a spoon:
'Come on in, Paddy Muldoon.'
And although I have never learned to swim
I would willingly have followed him.

Profumo

My mother had slapped a month-long news embargo
on his very name. The inhalation
of my first, damp
menthol fag behind the Junior Common Room.

The violet-scented Thirteenth Birthday card
to which I would affix a stamp
with the Queen's head upside down, swalk,
and post to Frances Hagan.

The spontaneously-combustible *News of the World*
under my mother's cushion
as she shifted from ham to snobbish ham;

'Haven't I told you, time and time again,
that you and she are chalk
and cheese? Away and read Masefield's 'Cargoes'.'

Christo's

Two workmen were carrying a sheet of asbestos
down the Main Street of Dingle;
it must have been nailed, at a slight angle,
to the same-sized gap between Brandon

and whichever's the next mountain.
Nine o'clock. We watched the village dogs
take turns to spritz the hotel's refuse-sacks.
I remembered Tralee's unbiodegradable flags

from the time of the hunger-strikes.
We drove all day past mounds of sugar-beet,
hay-stacks, silage-pits, building-sites,
a thatched cottage even –

all of them draped in black polythene
and weighted against the north-east wind
by concrete blocks, old tyres; bags of sand
at a makeshift army post

across the border. By the time we got to Belfast
the whole of Ireland would be under wraps
like, as I said, 'one of your man's landscapes'.
'Your man's? You don't mean Christo's?'

The Fox

Such an alarm
as was raised last night
by the geese
on John Mackle's goose-farm.

I got up and opened
the venetian blind.
You lay
three fields away

in Collegelands
graveyard, in ground
so wet you weren't so much
buried there as drowned.

That was a month ago.
I see your face
above its bib
pumped full of formaldehyde.

You seem engrossed,
as if I'd come on you
painfully writing your name
with a carpenter's pencil

on the lid
of a mushroom-box.
You're saying, *Go back to bed.*
It's only yon dog-fox.

The Soap-Pig

I must have been dozing in the tub
when the telephone
rang and a small, white grub
crawled along the line
and into my head:
Michael Heffernan was dead.

All I could think of
was his Christmas present
from what must have been 1975.
It squatted there on the wash-stand,
an amber, pig-shaped
bar of soap.

He had breezed into Belfast
in a three-quarter length coney-fur
to take up the post
of Drama Producer
with the still-reputable Beeb,
where I had somehow wangled a job.

Together we learned from Denys
Hawthorne and Allan McClelland
to float, like Saint Gennys,
on our own hands
through airwaves mostly jammed by cub-
reporters and poisoned pups.

He liked to listen at full tilt
to bootleg tapes
of Ian Paisley's assaults
on Papes,
regretful only that they weren't in quad.
His favourite word was *quidditas*.

I could just see the Jesuitical,
kitsch-camp slip-
knot in the tail
of even that bar of soap.
For this was Heffernan
saying, 'You stink to high heaven.'

Which I well knew. Many's an Arts Club
night with Barfield and Mason
ended with me throwing up
at the basin.
Anne-Marie looked on, her unspoken,
'That's to wash, not boke in.'

This, or any, form of self-regard
cut no ice
with Michael, who'd undergone heart-
surgery at least twice
while I knew him. On a trip
once to the Wexford slobs

he and I had shared
a hotel room. When he slipped
off his shirt

there were two unfashionably-broad lap-
els where the surgeons had sawn
through the xylophone

on which he liked to play
Chopin or *Chop-*
sticks until he was blue
in the face; be-bop, doo-wop:
they'd given him a tiny, plastic valve
that would, it seemed, no more dissolve

than the soap-pig I carried
on successive flits
from Marlborough Park (and Anne-Marie)
to the Malone Avenue flat
(*Chez Moy*, it was later dubbed)
to the rented house in Dub (as in *Dub-*

lin) Lane,
until, at last, in Landseer Street
Mary unpeeled its cellophane
and it landed on its feet
among porcelain, glass and heliotrope
pigs from all parts of the globe.

When we went on holiday to France
our house-sitter was troub-
led by an unearthly fragrance
at one particular step
on the landing. It was no pooka,
of course, but the camomile soap-pig

that Mary, in a fit of pique,
would later fling into the back yard.
As I unpicked
the anthracite-shards
from its body, I glimpsed the scrab-
nosed, condemned slab

of our sow that dropped
dead from a chill in 1966,
its uneven litter individually wrapped
in a banana box
with polystyrene and wood-shavings;
this time Mary was leaving,

taking with her the gold
and silver pigs, the ivory.
For Michael Heffernan, the common cold
was an uncommon worry
that might as easily have stopped
him in his tracks. He'd long since escaped

Belfast for London's dog-eat-dog
back-stab
and leap-frog.
More than once he collap-
sed at his desk. But Margaret
would steady him through the Secretariat

towards their favourite restaurant
where, given my natural funk
I think of as restraint,

I might have avoided that Irish drunk
whose slow jibes
Michael parried, but whose quick jab

left him forever at a loss for words.
For how he would delib-
erate on whether two six-foot boards
sealed whith ship's
varnish and two tea-chests
(another move) on which all this rests

is a table; or this merely a token
of some ur-chair,
or – being broken –
a chair at all: the mind's a razor
on the body's strop.
And the soap-pig? It's a bar of soap,

now the soap-sliver
in a flowered dish
that I work each morning into a lather
with my father's wobbling-brush,
then reconcile to its pool of glop
on my mother's wash-stand's marble top.

Something Else

When your lobster was lifted out of the tank
to be weighed
I thought of woad,
of madders, of fugitive, indigo inks,

of how Nerval
was given to promenade
a lobster on a gossamer thread,
how, when a decent interval

had passed
(*son front rouge encor du baiser de la reine*)
and his hopes of Adrienne

proved false,
he hanged himself from a lamp-post
with a length of chain, which made me think

of something else, then something else again.

Sushi

'Why do we waste so much time in arguing?'
We were sitting at the sushi-bar
drinking *Kirin* beer
and watching the Master chef
fastidiously shave
salmon, tuna and yellowtail
while a slightly more volatile
apprentice
fanned the rice,
every grain of which was magnetized
in one direction – east.
Then came translucent strips
of octopus,
squid and conger,
pickled ginger
and pale-green horseradish . . .
'It's as if you've some kind of death-wish.
You won't even talk . . .'
On the sidewalk
a woman in a leotard
with a real leopard
in tow.
For an instant I saw beyond the roe
of sea-urchins,
the erogenous
zones of shad and sea-bream;
I saw, when the steam
cleared, how this apprentice
had scrimshandered a rose's

exquisite petals
not from some precious metal
or wood or stone
('I might just as well be eating alone.')
but the tail-end of a carrot:
how when he submitted this work of art
to the Master –
Is it not the height of arrogance
to propose that God's no more arcane
than the smack of oregano,
orgone,
the inner organs
of beasts and fowls, the mines of Arigna,
the poems of Louis Aragon? –
it might have been alabaster
or jade
the Master so gravely weighed
from hand to hand
with the look of a man unlikely to confound
Duns Scotus, say, with Scotus Eriugena.

from 7, Middagh Street

This lobster's not a lobster but the telephone
that rang for Neville Chamberlain.

It droops from a bare branch
above a plate, on which the remains of lunch

include a snapshot of Hitler
and some boiled beans left over

from *Soft Construction: A Premonition
of Civil War*. When Breton

hauled me before his kangaroo-court
I quoted the Manifesto; we must disregard

moral and aesthetic considerations
for the integrity of our dream-visions.

What if I dreamed of Hitler as a masochist
who raises his fist

only to be beaten?
I might have dreamed of fucking André Breton

he so pooh-poohed my *Enigma of William Tell*.
There I have Lenin kneel

with one massive elongated buttock
and the elongated peak

of his cap supported by two forked sticks.
This time there's a raw beef-steak

on the son's head. My father croons a lullaby.
Is it that to refer, however obliquely,

is to refer? In October, 1934,
I left Barcelona by the back door

with a portfolio of work
for my first one-man show in New York.

A starry night. The howling of dogs.
The Anarchist taxi-driver carried two flags,

Spanish and Catalan. Which side was I on?
Not one, or both, or none.

I who had knelt with Lenin in Breton's court
and sworn allegiance to the proletariat

had seen the chasm
between myself and surrealism

begin as a hair-crack on a tile.
In *Soft Construction* I painted a giant troll

tearing itself apart limb
by outlandish limb.

Among the broken statues of Valladolid
there's one whose foot's still welded

to the granite plinth
from which, like us, it draws its strength.

From that, and from those few boiled beans.
We cannot gormandize upon

the flesh of Cain and Abel
without some melancholic vegetable

bringing us back to earth, to the boudoir
in the abattoir.

Our civil wars, the crumbling of empires,
the starry nights without number

safely under our belts,
have only slightly modified the tilt

of the acanthus leaf,
its spiky puce-and-alabaster an end in itself.

from MADOC: A MYSTERY

The Key

I ran into Foley six months ago in a dubbing suite in Los
Angeles. He was half-way through post-production on a
remake of *The Hoodlum Priest*, a film for which I've a special
affection since my cousin, Marina McCall, was an extra in the
first version. She had worked as a nanny for various movie
stars, including Tippi Hedren, and seemed to spend half her
time in the sky between New York and L.A. Though I sat
through three or four showings of *The Hoodlum Priest* in the
Olympic Cinema, Moy, and carefully scrutinized the crowd
scenes, I was never able to point to Marina with anything like
conviction.

Foley was working on a sequence involving a police line-up,
in which the victim shuffled along, stopped with each suspect
in turn, then shuffled on. At a critical moment, she dropped a
key on the floor. Foley was having trouble matching sound to
picture on this last effect. I was struck by the fact that, just as
early radio announcers had worn dinner-jackets, he was
wearing an ultramarine tuxedo. After half a dozen attempts,
he decided to call it quits, and emerged from his sound booth
like a diver from a bathyscope. He offered me a tidbit that
tasted only of mesquite.

I wanted to say something about Marina, something about
an 'identity parade' in which I once took part, something
about the etymology of 'tuxedo', but I found myself savouring
the play between 'booth' and 'bathy-', 'quits' and 'mesquite',
and began to 'misquote' myself;

> *When he sookied a calf down a boreen*
> *it was through Indo-European.*
> *When he clicked at a donkey carting dung*
> *your grandfather had an African tongue.*
> *You seem content to ventriloquize the surf.*

Foley swallowed whatever it was;

> *Still defending that same old patch of turf?*
> *Have you forgotten that 'hoodlum' is back-slang*
> *for the leader of a San Francisco street-gang?*

He flounced off into his cubicle. Though this, our only exchange, was remarkable for its banality, Foley has had some profound effect on me. These past six months I've sometimes run a little ahead of myself, but mostly I lag behind, my footfalls already pre-empted by their echoes.

Tea

I was rooting through tea-chest after tea-chest
as they drifted in along Key West

when I chanced on *Pythagoras in America*:
the book had fallen open at a book-mark

of tea; a tassel
of black watered silk from a Missal;

a tea-bird's black tail-feather.
All I have in the house is some left-over

squid cooked in its own ink
and this unfortunate cup of tea. Take it. Drink.

The Panther

For what it's worth, the last panther in Massachusetts
was brought to justice
in the woods beyond these meadows
and hung by its heels from a meat-hook
in what is now our kitchen.

(The house itself is something of a conundrum,
built as it was by an Ephraim Cowan from Antrim.)

I look in one evening while Jean
is jelly-making. She has rendered down pounds of grapes
and crab-apples
to a single jar
at once impenetrable and clear;
'Something's missing. This simply won't take.'

The air directly under the meat-hook —
it quakes, it quickens;
on a flagstone, the smudge of the tippy-tip of its nose.

Cauliflowers

Plants that glow in the dark have been developed
through gene-splicing, in which light-producing
bacteria from the mouths of fish are introduced to
cabbage, carrots and potatoes.

The National Enquirer

More often than not he stops at the headrig to light
his pipe
and try to regain
his composure. The price of cauliflowers
has gone down
two weeks in a row on the Belfast market.

From here we can just make out
a platoon of Light
Infantry going down
the road to the accompaniment of a pipe-
band. The sun glints on their silver-
buttoned jerkins.

My uncle, Patrick Regan,
has been leaning against the mud-guard
of the lorry. He levers
open the bonnet and tinkers with a light
wrench at the hose-pipe
that's always going down.

Then he himself goes down
to bleed oil into a jerry-can.
My father slips the pipe
into his scorch-marked
breast pocket and again makes light
of the trepanned cauliflowers.

All this as I listened to lovers
repeatedly going down
on each other in the next room . . . 'light
of my life . . .' in a motel in Oregon.
All this. Magritte's
pipe

and the pipe-
bomb. White Annetts. Gillyflowers.
Margaret,
are you grieving? My father going down
the primrose path with Patrick Regan.
All gone out of the world of light.

All gone down
the original pipe. And the cauliflowers
in an unmarked pit, that were harvested by their own light.

The Briefcase
for Seamus Heaney

I held the briefcase at arm's length from me;
the oxblood or liver
eelskin with which it was covered
had suddenly grown supple.

I'd been waiting in line for the cross-town
bus when an almighty cloudburst
left the sidewalk a raging torrent.

And though it contained only the first
inkling of this poem, I knew I daren't
set the briefcase down
to slap my pockets for an obol –

for fear it might slink into a culvert
and strike out along the East River
for the sea. By which I mean the 'open' sea.

from Madoc: A Mystery

VICO

A hand-wringing, small, grey squirrel
plods
along a wicker

treadmill that's attached
by an elaborate
system of levers

and cogs and cranks
and pulleys
and gears

and cams and cinches
and sprags and sprockets
and spindles

and tappets and trundles
and spirochetes
and winches

and jennies and jiggers
and pawls
and pranks

and the whole palaver
of rods
and ratchets

to a wicker
treadmill in which there plods
a hand-wringing, small, grey squirrel.

The Workmen's Chorus

When I woke up this morning, I was still in my dungarees.
I steadied myself at the washstand with a shot of Tanqueray.

Hand me up my spirit-level, my plumb-line and my plumb.
Hand me up my spirit-level, or I'll lose my equilibrium.

When the whistle blew at lunchtime, I opened my lunch-pail.
It was completely empty. That's why my mouth is full of nails.

My mother was a Mohawk, my father used to stay out nights.
That must be why I'm blessed with such a head for heights.

I'd sawn half-way through a plank. Now I can't see my mark.
It's the fate of every carpenter to fade into his own woodwork.

The Reporters' Quartet

When all's said and done we'd like to know
if Amundsen had reached the Pole.
Has he been struck some cruel blow?
Is he eaten by a whale?
Has he stumbled through a hole?
Is he lying at the bottom of the sea?
Going down,
going down,
going down in history.

At the end of the day we'd like to hear
some word on the anarchist plot
to kill the Emperor
of Japan. How goes it with the suffragettes?
Why was Canalejas shot?
Is China still our cup of tea?
Going down,
going down,
going down in history.

Nineteen twelve. The Greeks and Turks
fight a familiar duel.
The Piltdown Men of Planter stock
scuttle Irish Home Rule.
The *Titanic* founders on a berg.
The passengers cry wee-wee-wee.
Going down,
going down,
going down in history.

Nineteen thirteen. By now Niels Bohr
has cracked the atom's nut.
The Mexican Prime Minister
and the King of Greece are shot.
New leaders roll off the conveyor
belt like Henry Ford's first Model Ts.
Going down,
going down,
going down in history.

Nineteen fourteen. The latest news
has Woodrow Wilson's
warships pounding Veracruz.
All going down. All going down.
Though it's been five years since he fell off a mule
at the San Carlos agency,
Geronimo's still going down,
going down,
going down in history.

June twenty-eighth. As the guests arrive
for a soiree at Taliesin,
a shot rings out in Sarajevo.
Little do they think of the repercussions
as Archduke Franz Ferdinand,
Crown Prince of Austria,
goes down,
goes down,
goes down in history.

The Chef's Aria

I am a breast without a nipple.
I am a watch-tower without a beacon.
I am the gall in an oak-apple.
I am a birch stripped of its bark.
I am a raven swooping over the squadron.
I am a hang-nail on a finger.
I am the eye that looks askance.
I am a flint that holds no spark.
I am a half-moon-shaped gold torc.
I am a sponge steeped in vinegar.
I am the hart. I am the hind.
I am the green and burning tree.
I am the cloud no bigger than a hand.
I will go down in history.

The more I think of it, the more I've come to love
the tidal marshes of Hackensack,
the planes stacked
over Newark, even the smell of cloves

and chloroform
that sweetens Elizabeth.
(At Exit 9, the man in the toll-booth
almost lost an arm

to Oscar MacOscair, as we call the hound . . .)
The more I think of it, the less I'm clear
as to why U2 should spend a year
remaking themselves as a garage band.

Which reminds me; we must see the new Wim Wenders.
In the meantime, let's rent *Pathfinder*.

§

The Feast of the Epiphany. It's been so mild
the bell of millet
strung up for the finches
is all but dumb: a few inches

of snow, one hard frost,
might draw the deer out of the forest
to prune the vines
from the picket fence

or vault the five-foot chicken-wire cordon
round our herb-garden.
In the meantime, my lemon-peel

and bacon-rind mobile
is losing something of its verve.
I wait in vain for some small showing forth.

§

Only a few weeks ago, the sonogram of Jean's womb
resembled nothing so much
as a satellite map of Ireland:

now the image
is so well-defined we can make out not only a hand
but a thumb;

on the road to Spiddal, a woman hitching a ride;
a gladiator in his net, passing judgement on the crowd.

§

After two days grading papers from the seminar I taught
on Swift, Yeats, Sterne,
Joyce, and Beckett,
I break my sword across my iron knee:

in the long sonata of *The Dead*
ceremony's a name for the rich horn –
these images fresh images beget –
and custom for the hardy laurel tree;

for the gravel was thrown up against the window-pane
not by Michael Furey but the Dean
who stepped on to an outward-bound tram

and embarked on *Immram Curaig Mael Duin*,
while the Butler that withstood beside the brackish Boyne
was one James Butler, Corporal Trim.

§

Not for nothing would I versify
'The Alchemist and Barrister', rhyme (*pace* Longley) 'cat'
with 'dog', expand on the forsythia
that graces our back door: 'humdrum', 'inadequate',

'inconsequential journalese', 'a klieg light
masquerading as the moon'; none will,
I trust, look for a pattern in this crazy quilt
where all is random, 'all so trivial',

unless it be Erasmus, unless
Erasmus again steel
himself as his viscera are cranked out by a windlass

yard upon 'xanthous' yard;
again to steel himself, then somehow to exhort
the windlass-men to even greater zeal.

§

I look out the kitchen window. A cigarette burns
in the midst of the pyracanthus:
'What's with you, *a mhic*?
Apart from the "eel-grass and bladderwrack"

there's not an image here that's worth a fuck.
Who gives a shit about the dreck
of your life? Who gives a toss
about your tossing off?' 'I know, I know, but . . .'

'But nothing: you know it's dross;
you know that "Erasmus" stuff is an inept
attempt to cover your arse;

leave off your laundry-lists and tax-returns
and go back to making metaphors . . .'
Something in that 'go back' reminds me of Xanthus.

§

With that the horse-head folds his horse-hide parachute
till it's no bigger than a glove:

he slaps my cheek; 'Above all else, you must atone
for everything you've said and done

against your mother: meet excess of love
with excess of love; begin on the Feast of Saint Brigid.'

Brazil

When my mother snapped open her flimsy parasol
it was Brazil: if not Brazil,

then Uruguay.
One nipple darkening her smock.

My shame-faced *Tantum Ergo*
struggling through thurified smoke.

*

Later that afternoon would find
me hunched over the font

as she rinsed my hair. Her towel-turban.
Her terrapin

comb scuttling under the faucet.
I stood there in my string vest

and shorts while she repeated, '*Champi . . . ?*
Champi . . . ? Champi . . . ?' Then,

that bracelet of shampoo
about the bone, her triumphant '*ChampiÑON*'.

*

If not Uruguay, then Ecuador:
it must be somewhere on or near the equator

given how water
plunged headlong into water

when she pulled the plug.
So much for the obliq-

uity of leaving *What a Boy Should Know*
under my pillow: now *vagina* and *vas*

deferens made a holy show
of themselves. 'There is inherent vice

in everything,' as O'Higgins
would proclaim: it was O'Higgins who duly

had the terms 'widdershins'
and 'deasil' expunged from the annals of Chile.

Oscar

Be that as it may, I'm wakened by the moans
not of the wind
nor the wood-demons

but Oscar MacOscair, as we call the hound
who's wangled himself
into our bed: 'Why?' 'Why not?'

He lies between us like an ancient quoof
with a snout of perished gutta-
percha, and whines at something on the roof.

*

I'm suddenly mesmerized
by what I saw only today: a pair of high heels
abandoned on the road to Amherst.

*

And I've taken off, over the towns of Keady
and Aughnacloy and Caledon —
Et in Arcadia —

to a grave lit by acetylene
in which, though she preceded him
by a good ten years, my mother's skeleton

has managed to worm
its way back on top of the old man's,
and she once again has him under her thumb.

Milkweed and Monarch

As he knelt by the grave of his mother and father
the taste of dill, or tarragon –
he could barely tell one from the other –

filled his mouth. It seemed as if he might smother.
Why should he be stricken
with grief, not for his mother and father,

but a woman slinking from the fur of a sea-otter
in Portland, Maine, or, yes, Portland, Oregon –
he could barely tell one from the other –

and why should he now savour
the tang of her, her little pickled gherkin,
as he knelt by the grave of his mother and father?

*

He looked about. He remembered her palaver
on how both earth and sky would darken –
'You could barely tell one from the other' –

while the Monarch butterflies passed over
in their milkweed-hunger: 'A wing-beat, some reckon,
may trigger off the mother and father

of all storms, striking your Irish Cliffs of Moher
with the force of a hurricane.'
Then: 'Milkweed and Monarch "invented" each other.'

*

He looked about. Cow's-parsley in a samovar.
He'd mistaken his mother's name, 'Regan', for 'Anger':
as he knelt by the grave of his mother and father
he could barely tell one from the other.

Twice

It was so cold last night the water in the barrel grew a sod
of water: I asked Taggart and McAnespie to come over
and we sawed and sawed
for half an hour until, using a crowbar as a lever

in the way Archimedes always said
would shift the balance, we were somehow able to manoeuvre
out and, finally, stand on its side
in the snow that fifteen- or eighteen-inch thick manhole cover.

That 'manhole cover' was surely no more ice
than are McAnespie and Taggart still of this earth;
when I squinnied through it I saw 'Lefty' Clery, *An Ciotach*,

grinning from both ends of the school photograph,
having jooked behind the three-deep rest of us to meet the
     Kodak's
leisurely pan; 'Two places at once, was it, or one place twice?'

Footling

This I don't believe: rather than take a header
off the groyne
and into the ground swell,
yea verily, the *ground swell* of life,

she shows instead her utter
disregard – part diffidence, but mostly scorn –
for what lies behind the great sea-wall
and what knocks away at the great sea-cliff;

though she's been in training all spring and summer
and swathed herself in fat
and Saran-

Wrap like an old-time Channel swimmer,
she's now got cold feet
and turned in on herself, the phantom 'a' in Cesarian.

The Birth

Seven o'clock. The seventh day of the seventh month of the
    year.
No sooner have I got myself up in lime-green scrubs,
a sterile cap and mask,
and taken my place at the head of the table

than the windlass-women ply their shears
and gralloch-grub
for a footling foot, then, warming to their task,
haul into the inestimable

realm of apple-blossoms and chanterelles and damsons and
    eel-spears
and foxes and the general hubbub
of inkies and jennets and Kickapoos with their lemniscs
or peekaboo-quiffs of Russian sable

and tallow-unctuous vernix, into the realm of the widgeon —
the 'whew' or 'yellow-poll', not the 'zuizin' —

Dorothy Aoife Korelitz Muldoon: I watch through floods of
    tears
as they give her a quick rub-a-dub
and whisk
her off to the nursery, then check their staple-guns for staples.

Cows

for Dermot Seymour

Even as we speak, there's a smoker's cough
from behind the whitethorn hedge: we stop dead in our tracks;
a distant tingle of water into a trough.

*

In the past half-hour – since a cattle-truck
all but sent us shuffling off this mortal coil –
we've consoled ourselves with the dregs

of a bottle of Redbreast. Had Hawthorne been a Gael,
I insist, the scarlet 'A' on Hester Prynne
would have stood for 'Alcohol'.

*

This must be the same truck whose tail-lights burn
so dimly, as if caked with dirt,
three or four hundred yards along the boreen

(a diminutive form of the Gaelic *bóthar*, 'a road',
from *bó*, 'a cow', and *thar*
meaning, in this case, something like 'athwart',

'boreen' has entered English 'through the air'
despite the protestations of the O.E.D.):
why, though, should one tail-light flash and flare,

then flicker-fade
to an after-image of tourmaline
set in a dark part-jet, part-jasper or -jade?

*

That smoker's cough again: it triggers off from drumlin
to drumlin an emphysemantiphon
of cows. They hoist themselves on to their trampoline

and steady themselves and straight away divine
water in some far-flung spot
to which they then gravely incline. This is no Devon

cow-coterie, by the way, whey-faced, with Spode
hooves and horns: nor are they the metaphysicattle of Japan
that have merely to anticipate

scoring a bull's-eye and, lo, it happens;
these are earth-flesh, earth-blood, salt of the earth,
whose talismans are their own jaw-bones

buried under threshold and hearth.
For though they trace themselves to the kith and kine
that presided over the birth

of Christ (so carry their calves a full nine
months and boast liquorice
cachous on their tongues), they belong more to the line

that's tramped these cwms and corries
since Cuchulainn tramped Aoife.
Again the flash. Again the fade. However I might allegorize

some oscaraboscarabinary bevy
of cattle there's no getting round this cattle-truck,
one light on the blink, laden with what? Microwaves? Hi-fis?

*

Oscaraboscarabinary: a twin, entwined, a tree, a Tuareg;
a double dung-beetle; a plain
and simple hi-firing party; an off-the-back-of-a-lorry drogue?

Enough of Colette and Céline, Céline and Paul Celan:
enough of whether Nabokov
taught at Wellesley or Wesleyan.

Now let us talk of slaughter and the slain,
the helicopter gun-ship, the mighty Kalashnikov:
let's rest for a while in a place where a cow has lain.

from Yarrow

In a conventional tornada, the strains of her '*Che sera, sera*'
or 'The Harp That Once' would transport me back
to a bath resplendent with yarrow

(it's really a sink set on breeze- or cinder-blocks):
then I might be delivered
from the rail's monotonous 'alack, alack';

in a conventional envoy, her voice would be ever
soft, gentle and low   .
and the chrism of milfoil might over-

flow
as the great wheel
came full circle; here a bittern's bibulous '*Orinochone O*'

is counterpointed only by that corncrake, by the gulder-gowl
of a nightjar, I guess, above the open-cast mines,
by a quail's

indecipherable code; of the great cog-wheel, all that remains
is a rush of air – a wing-beat,
more like – past my head; even as I try to regain

my equilibrium, there's no more relief, no more respite
than when I scurried, click, down McParland's lane
with my arms crossed, click, under my armpits;

I can no more read between the lines
of the quail's 'Wet-my-lips' or his 'Quick, quick'
than get to grips with Friedrich Hölderlin

or that phrase in Vallejo having to do with the 'ache'
in his forearms; on the freshly-laid asphalt
a freshly-peeled willow-switch, or baton, shows a vivid mosaic

of gold on a black field, while over the fields
of buckwheat it's harder and harder to pin down a gowk's
poopookarian *ignis fatuus*;

though it slips, the great cog,
there's something about the quail's 'Wet-my-foot'
and the sink full of hart's-tongue, borage and common kedlock

that I've either forgotten or disavowed;
it has to do with a trireme, laden with ravensara,
that was lost with all hands between Ireland and Montevideo.

Incantata

In memory of Mary Farl Powers

I thought of you tonight, *a leanbh*, lying there in your long
    barrow
colder and dumber than a fish by Francisco de Herrera,
as I X-Actoed from a spud the Inca
glyph for a mouth: thought of that first time I saw your pink
spotted torso, distant-near as a nautilus,
when you undid your portfolio, yes indeedy,
and held the print of what looked like a cankered potato
at arm's length — your arms being longer, it seemed, than
    Lugh's.

Even Lugh of the Long (sometimes the Silver) Arm
would have wanted some distance between himself and the
    army-worms
that so clouded the sky over St Cloud you'd have to seal
the doors and windows and steel
yourself against their nightmarish *déjeuner sur l'herbe*:
try as you might to run a foil
across their tracks, it was to no avail;
the army-worms shinnied down the stove-pipe on an
    army-worm rope.

I can hardly believe that, when we met, my idea of 'R and R'
was to get smashed, almost every night, on sickly-sweet
    Demerara
rum and Coke: as well as leaving you a grass widow
(remember how Krapp looks up 'viduity'?),
after eight or ten or twelve of those dark rums
it might be eight or ten or twelve o'clock before I'd land
back home in Landseer Street, deaf and blind
to the fact that not only was I all at sea, but in the doldrums.

Again and again you'd hold forth on your own version
    of Thomism,
your own *Summa*
Theologiae that in everything there is an order,
that the things of the world sing out in a great oratorio:
it was Thomism, though, tempered by *La Nausée*,
by His Nibs Sam Bethicket,
and by that Dublin thing, that an artist must walk down
    Baggott
Street wearing a hair-shirt under the shirt of Nessus.

'*D'éirigh me ar maidin*,' I sang, '*a tharraingt chun aoinigh
    mhóir*':
our first night, you just had to let slip that your secret amour
for a friend of mine was such
that you'd ended up lying with him in a ditch
under a bit of whin, or gorse, or furze,
somewhere on the border of Leitrim, perhaps, or Roscommon:
'gamine,' I wanted to say, 'kimono';
even then it was clear I'd never be at the centre of your
    universe.

[166]

Nor should I have been, since you were there already, your
   own *Ding*
an sich, no less likely to take wing
than the Christ you drew for a Christmas card as a pupa
in swaddling clothes: and how resolutely you would
   pooh pooh
the idea I shared with Vladimir and Estragon,
with whom I'd been having a couple of jars,
that this image of the Christ-child swaddled and laid in the
   manger
could be traced directly to those army-worm dragoons.

I thought of the night Vladimir was explaining to all and
   sundry
the difference between *geantrai* and *suantrai*
and you remarked on how you used to have a crush
on Burt Lancaster as Elmer Gantry, and Vladimir went to
   brush
the ash off his sleeve with a legerdemain
that meant only one thing – 'Why does he put up with this
   crap?' –
and you weighed in with 'To live in a dustbin, eating scrap,
seemed to Nagg and Nell a most eminent domain.'

How little you were exercised by those tiresome literary
   intrigues,
how you urged me to have no more truck
than the Thane of Calder
with a fourth estate that professes itself to be '*égalitaire*'
but wants only blood on the sand: yet, irony of ironies,
you were the one who, in the end,
got yourself up as a *retiarius* and, armed with net and trident,
marched from Mount Street to the Merrion Square arena.

In the end, you were the one who went forth to beard the lion,
you who took the DART line
every day from Jane's flat in Dun Laoghaire, or Dalkey,
dreaming your dream that the subterranean Dodder and Tolka
might again be heard above the *hoi polloi*
for whom Irish 'art' means a High Cross at Carndonagh or
    Corofin
and *The Book of Kells*: not until the lion cried craven
would the poor Tolka and the poor Dodder again sing out
    for joy.

I saw you again tonight, in your jump-suit, thin as a rake,
your hand moving in such a deliberate arc
as you ground a lithographic stone
that your hand and the stone blurred to one
and your face blurred into the face of your mother, Betty
    Wahl,
who took your failing, ink-stained hand
in her failing, ink-stained hand
and together you ground down that stone by sheer force of
    will.

I remember your pooh poohing, as we sat there on the
    'Enterprise',
my theory that if your name is Powers
you grow into it or, at least,
are less inclined to tremble before the likes of this bomb-blast
further up the track: I myself was shaking like a leaf
as we wondered whether the I.R.A. or the Red
Hand Commandos or even the Red
Brigades had brought us to a standstill worthy of Hamm
    and Clov.

Hamm and Clov; Nagg and Nell; Watt and Knott;
the fact is that we'd been at a standstill long before the night
things came to a head,
long before we'd sat for half the day in the sweltering heat
somewhere just south of Killnasaggart
and I let slip a name – her name – off my tongue
and you turned away (I see it now) the better to deliver
        the sting
in your own tail, to let slip your own little secret.

I thought of you again tonight, thin as a rake, as you bent
over the copper plate of 'Emblements',
its tidal wave of army-worms into which you all but
        disappeared:
I wanted to catch something of its spirit
and yours, to body out your disembodied *vox
clamantis in deserto*, to let this all-too-cumbersome device
of a potato-mouth in a potato-face
speak out, unencumbered, from its long, low, mould-filled
        box.

I wanted it to speak to what seems always true of the truly
        great,
that you had a winningly inaccurate
sense of your own worth, that you would second-guess
yourself too readily by far, that you would rally to any cause
before your own, mine even,
though you detected in me a tendency to put
on too much artificiality, both as man and poet,
which is why you called me 'Polyester' or 'Polyurethane'.

That last time in Dublin, I copied with a quill dipped in
     oak-gall
onto a sheet of vellum, or maybe a human caul,
a poem for *The Great Book of Ireland*: as I watched the low
swoop over the lawn today of a swallow
I thought of your animated talk of Camille Pissarro
and André Derain's *The Turning Road, L'Estaque:*
when I saw in that swallow's nest a face in a mud-pack
from that muddy road I was filled again with a profound
     sorrow.

You must have known already, as we moved from the
     'Hurly Burly'
to McDaid's or Riley's,
that something was amiss: I think you even mentioned a
     homeopath
as you showed off the great new acid-bath
in the Graphic Studio, and again undid your portfolio
to lay out your latest works; I try to imagine the strain
you must have been under, pretending to be as right as rain
while hearing the bells of a church from some long-flooded
     valley.

From the Quabbin reservoir, maybe, where the banks and
     bakeries
of a dozen little submerged Pompeii reliquaries
still do a roaring trade: as clearly as I saw your death-mask
in that swallow's nest, you must have heard the music
rise from the muddy ground between
your breasts as a nocturne, maybe, by John Field;
to think that you thought yourself so invulnerable, so
     inviolate,
that a little cancer could be beaten.

You must have known, as we walked through the ankle-deep
        clabber
with Katherine and Jean and the long-winded Quintus
        Calaber,
that cancer had already made such a breach
that you would almost surely perish:
you must have thought, as we walked through the woods
along the edge of the Quabbin,
that rather than let some doctor cut you open
you'd rely on infusions of hardock, hemlock, all the idle
        weeds.

I thought again of how art may be made, as it was by
        André Derain,
of nothing more than a turn
in the road where a swallow dips into the mire
or plucks a strand of bloody wool from a strand of barbed wire
in the aftermath of Chickamauga or Culloden
and builds from pain, from misery, from a deep-seated hurt,
a monument to the human heart
that shines like a golden dome among roofs rain-glazed
        and leaden.

I wanted the mouth in this potato-cut
to be heard far beyond the leaden, rain-glazed roofs of Quito,
to be heard all the way from the southern hemisphere
to Clontarf or Clondalkin, to wherever your sweet-severe
spirit might still find a toe-hold
in this world: it struck me then how you would be aghast
at the thought of my thinking you were some kind of ghost
who might still roam the earth in search of an earthly delight.

You'd be aghast at the idea of your spirit hanging over this vale
of tears like a jump-suited jump-jet whose vapour-trail
unravels a sky: for there's nothing, you'd say, nothing over
and above the sky itself, nothing but cloud-cover
reflected in a thousand lakes; it seems that Minne-
sota itself means 'sky-tinted water', that the sky is a great slab
of granite or iron ore that might at any moment slip
back into the worked-out sky-quarry, into the worked-out
    sky-mines.

To use the word 'might' is to betray you once too often,
   to betray
your notion that nothing's random, nothing arbitrary:
the gelignite weeps, the hands fly by on the alarm clock,
the 'Enterprise' goes clackety-clack
as they all must; even the car hijacked that morning in
    the Cross,
that was preordained, its owner spread on the bonnet
before being gagged and bound or bound
and gagged, that was fixed like the stars in the Southern Cross.

The fact that you were determined to cut yourself off in your
    prime
because it was *pre*-determined has my eyes abrim:
I crouch with Belacqua
and Lucky and Pozzo in the Acacacac-
ademy of Anthropopopometry, trying to make sense of the
    '*quaquaqua*'
of that potato-mouth; that mouth as prim
and proper as it's full of self-opprobrium,
with its '*quaquaqua*', with its 'Quoiquoiquoiquoiquoiquoi-
    quoiq'.

That's all that's left of the voice of Enrico Caruso
from all that's left of an opera-house somewhere in Matto
    Grosso,
all that's left of the hogweed and horehound and cuckoo-pint,
of the eighteen soldiers dead at Warrenpoint,
of the Black Church clique and the Graphic Studio claque,
of the many moons of glasses on a tray,
of the brewery-carts drawn by moon-booted drays,
of those jump-suits worn under your bottle-green worsted
    cloak.

Of the great big dishes of chicken lo mein and beef chow mein,
of what's mine is yours and what's yours mine,
of the oxlips and cowslips
on the banks of the Liffey at Leixlip
where the salmon breaks through the either/or neither/nor
    nether
reaches despite the temple-veil
of itself being rent and the penny left out overnight on the rail
is a sheet of copper when the mail-train has passed over.

Of the bride carried over the threshold, hey, only to alight
on the limestone slab of another threshold,
of the swarm, the cast,
the colt, the spew of bees hanging like a bottle of Lucozade
from a branch the groom must sever,
of Emily Post's ruling, in *Etiquette*,
on how best to deal with the butler being in cahoots
with the cook when they're both in cahoots with the chauffeur.

Of that poplar-flanked stretch of road between Leiden
and The Hague, of the road between Rathmullen and
    Ramelton,
where we looked so long and hard
for some trace of Spinoza or Amelia Earhart,
both of them going down with their engines on fire:
of the stretch of road somewhere near Urney
where Orpheus was again overwhelmed by that urge to turn
back and lost not only Eurydice but his steel-strung lyre.

Of the sparrows and finches in their bell of suet,
of the bitter-sweet
bottle of Calvados we felt obliged to open
somewhere near Falaise, so as to toast our new-found *copains*,
of the priest of the parish
who came enquiring about our 'status', of the hedge-clippers
I somehow had to hand, of him running like the clappers
up Landseer Street, of my subsequent self-reproach.

Of the remnants of Airey Neave, of the remnants of
    Mountbatten,
of the famous *andouilles*, of the famous *boudins
noirs et blancs*, of the barrel-vault
of the Cathedral at Rouen, of the flashlight, fat and roll of felt
on each of their sledges, of the music
of Joseph Beuys's pack of huskies, of that baldy little bugger
mushing them all the way from Berncastel through Bacarrat
to Belfast, his head stuck with honey and gold-leaf like a
    mosque.

Of Benjamin Britten's *Lachrymae*, with its gut-wrenching
	viola,
of Vivaldi's *Four Seasons*, of Frankie Valli's,
of Braque's great painting *The Shower of Rain*,
of the fizzy, lemon or sherbet-green *Ranus ranus*
plonked down in Trinity like a little Naugahyde pouffe,
of eighteen soldiers dead in Oriel,
of the weakness for a little fol-de-rol-de-rolly
suggested by the gap between the front teeth of the Wife
	of Bath.

Of *A Sunday Afternoon on the Island of La Grande Jatte*,
	of Seurat's
piling of tesserae upon tesserae
to give us a monkey arching its back
and the smoke arching out from a smoke-stack,
of Sunday afternoons in the Botanic Gardens, going with
	the flow
of the burghers of Sandy Row and Donegal
Pass and Andersonstown and Rathcoole,
of the army Landrover flaunt-flouncing by with its heavy
	furbelow.

Of Marlborough Park, of Notting Hill, of the Fitzroy Avenue
immortalized by Van 'His real name's Ivan'
Morrison, 'and him the dead spit
of Padraic Fiacc', of John Hewitt, the famous expat,
in whose memory they offer every year six of their best milch
	cows,
of the Bard of Ballymacarrett,
of every ungodly poet in his or her godly garret,
of Medhbh and Michael and Frank and Ciaran and 'wee'
	John Qughes.

Of the Belfast school, so called, of the school of hard knocks,
of your fervent eschewal of stockings and socks
as you set out to hunt down your foes
as implacably as the *tóraidheacht* through the Fews
of Redmond O'Hanlon, of how that 'd' and that 'c' aspirate
in *tóraidheacht* make it sound like a last gasp in an
    oxygen-tent,
of your refusal to open a vent
but to breathe in spirit of salt, the mordant salt-spirit.

Of how mordantly hydrochloric acid must have scored and
    scarred,
of the claim that boiled skirrets
can cure the spitting of blood, of that dank
flat somewhere off Morehampton Road, of the unbelievable
    stink
of valerian or feverfew simmering over a low heat,
of your sitting there, pale and gaunt,
with that great prescriber of boiled skirrets, Dr John
    Arbuthnot,
your face in a bowl of feverfew, a towel over your head.

Of the great roll of paper like a bolt of cloth
running out again and again like a road at the edge of a cliff,
of how you called a Red Admiral a Red
Admirable, of how you were never in the red
on either the first or the last
of the month, of your habit of loosing the drawstring of
    your purse
and finding one scrunched-up, obstreperous
note and smoothing it out and holding it up, pristine and
    pellucid.

Of how you spent your whole life with your back to the wall,
of your generosity when all the while
you yourself lived from hand
to mouth, of Joseph Beuys's pack of hounds
crying out from their felt and fat 'Atone, atone, atone',
of Watt remembering the '*Krak! Krek! Krik!*'
of those three frogs' karaoke
like the still, sad, *basso continuo* of the great quotidian.

Of a ground bass of sadness, yes, but also a sennet of hautboys
as the fat and felt hounds of Beuys O'Beuys
bayed at the moon over a caravan
in Dunmore East, I'm pretty sure it was, or Dungarvan:
of my guest appearance in your self-portrait not as a hidalgo
from a long line
of hidalgos but a hound-dog, a *leanbh*,
a dog that skulks in the background, a dog that skulks and
    stalks.

Of that self-portrait, of the self-portraits by Rembrandt van
    Rijn,
of all that's revelation, all that's rune,
of all that's composed, all composed of odds and ends,
of that daft urge to make amends
when it's far too late, too late even to make sense of the clutter
of false trails and reversed horseshoe tracks
and the aniseed we took it in turn to drag
across each other's scents, when only a fish is dumber and
    colder.

Of your avoidance of canned goods, in the main,
on account of the exceeeeeeeeeeeeeeeeedingly high risk of
    ptomaine,
of corned beef in particular being full of crap,
of your delight, so, in eating a banana as ceremoniously
    as Krapp
but flinging the skin over your shoulder like a thrush
flinging off a shell from which it's only just managed to disinter
a snail, like a stone-faced, twelfth-century
FitzKrapp eating his banana by the mellow, yellow light of a
    rush.

Of the 'Yes, let's go' spoken by Monsieur Tarragon,
of the early-ripening jardonelle, the tumorous jardon,
    the jargon
of jays, the jars
of tomato relish and the jars
of Victoria plums, absolutely *de rigueur* for a passable
    plum baba,
of the drawers full of balls of twine and butcher's string,
of Dire Straits playing 'The Sultans of Swing',
of the horse's hock suddenly erupting in those boils and
    buboes.

Of the Greek figurine of a pig, of the pig on a terracotta frieze,
of the sow dropping dead from some mysterious virus,
of your predilection for gammon
served with a sauce of coriander or cumin,
of the slippery elm, of the hornbeam or witch-, or even wych-,
hazel that's good for stopping a haemor-
rhage in mid-flow, of the merest of mere
hints of elderberry curing everything from sciatica to a stitch.

Of the decree *condemnator*, the decree *absolvitor*, the decree *nisi*,
of *Aosdána*, of *an chraobh cnuais*,
of the fields of buckwheat
taken over by garget, inkberry, scoke – all names for
     pokeweed –
of *Mother Courage*, of *Arturo Ui*,
of those Sunday mornings spent picking at sesame
noodles and all sorts and conditions of dim sum,
of tea and ham sandwiches in the Nesbitt Arms hotel in
     Ardara.

Of the day your father came to call, of your leaving your
     sick-room
in what can only have been a state of delirium,
of how you simply wouldn't relent
from your vision of a blind
watch-maker, of your fatal belief that fate
governs everything from the honey-rust of your father's
     terrier's
eyebrows to the horse that rusts and rears
in the furrow, of the furrows from which we can no more
     deviate

than they can from themselves, no more than the map of
     Europe
can be redrawn, than that Hermes might make a harp from
     his *harpe*,
than that we must live in a vale
of tears on the banks of the Lagan or the Foyle,
than that what we have is a done deal,
than that the Irish Hermes,
Lugh, might have leafed through his vast herbarium
for the leaf that had it within it, Mary, to anoint and anneal,

[179]

than that Lugh of the Long Arm might have found in the midst
        of *lus*
na leac or *lus na treatha* or *Frannc-lus*,
in the midst of eyebright, or speedwell, or tansy, an antidote,
than that this *Incantata*
might have you look up from your plate of copper or zinc
on which you've etched the row upon row
of army-worms, than that you might reach out, arrah,
and take in your ink-stained hands my own hands stained
        with ink.

Index of Titles